CONTENTS

Whither Sunday Trading?
The Case for Deregulation

JOHN BURTON
Professor of Business Administration
Birmingham Business School
University of Birmingham

Published by

INSTITUTE OF ECONOMIC AFFAIRS

First published in December 1993

by

THE INSTITUTE OF ECONOMIC AFFAIRS

2 Lord North Street, Westminster,

London SW1P 3LB

Hobart Paper 123

ISSN 0073-2818

ISBN 0-255 36328-1

Printed in Great Britain by

GORON PRO-PRINT CO LTD

6 Marlborough Road, Churchill Industrial Estate, Lancing, W. Sussex

Text set in Baskerville 11 on 12 point

FOREWORD

For many years there appears to have been widespread
agreement that the law which governs Sunday trading in
England and Wales should be reformed. Anomalies abound,
despite attempts to clarify the law both in British courts and in
the European Court of Justice. The law is applied differently
in different localities. Many shops now open on Sundays in
apparent defiance of the law and are well patronised by a
public evidently keen to shop on Sundays. Curiously, in
perhaps the biggest anomaly of all, the law in Scotland is
different, permitting trading on Sundays.

In *Hobart Paper* No.123, Professor John Burton of the
University of Birmingham considers why it is that, despite
apparent agreement that reform is needed, attempts to
change the legislation always seem to founder in the House of
Commons. Coincidentally, at about the time this *Paper* is
published, another series of Parliamentary discussions on
Sunday trading reform will begin.

In Burton's view, it is the power of organised producer
groups which obstructs sensible measures of reform. In his
words, '...numerous attempts to reform this chaotic
regulatory situation have been held in a gridlock ... most
importantly by the clash of organised sectional interests'
(Section II, p.26). As in so many other areas of economic
activity, organised producers are able to exercise disproportionate influence as compared with unorganised
consumers.

The main options for reform, supported by organised
groups, would open up new anomalies, according to Burton.
It is not possible to foresee developments in retailing and
specify them in legislation. Inevitably, '...regulations with
exemptions based on specified goods stipulated at a point in
time ... must fall into *ever-increasing* disrepair and disrepute
with the passage of time' (Section V, p.61). Moreover,
different producer groups will support different options for
'reform' because they expect thereby to gain a competitive
advantage:

> '... *any* regulatory scheme will ... give certain businesses artificial
> competitive advantages, whilst subjecting others to an imposed
> competitive hobble.' (Section V, p.64)

[7]

Professor Burton is firmly in favour of complete deregulation – 'Shoppers and shop managers would simply decide whether or not to engage in trading on Sundays' (Section V, p.52). He dismisses the concerns sometimes expressed that small shops would not survive, that there would be serious spillover effects from extra noise and congestion, and that employees would be adversely affected. He points out that present restrictions are widely regarded as outdated, that they are flouted, and that opinion polls show large majorities in favour of their abandonment.

His case rests ultimately on a general principle – that the criminal law '...should *not* be applied to mundane transactions between willing participants in which no public harm is involved' (Section VII, p.88). Such transactions should therefore, he concludes, be decriminalised: 'It is no part of the state's job in a free society to interfere with these transactions – let alone apply to them the full weight of the criminal law' (Section VII, p.88).

The views expressed in this *Hobart Paper* are those of the author, not of the Institute (which has no corporate view), its Trustees, Directors or Advisers. It is published in order to widen the framework within which Sunday trading is discussed.

December 1993   COLIN ROBINSON
Editorial Director, Institute of Economic Affairs;
Professor of Economics, University of Surrey

THE AUTHOR

JOHN BURTON is Professor of Business Administration at the Birmingham Business School, University of Birmingham, having previously held professorial appointments at the Leeds Business School and the European Business School, and also lecturing appointments with the Universities of Southampton and Birmingham, Kingston Polytechnic, and Boston University. From 1984-87 he was Research Director at the Institute of Economic Affairs, and in 1987 also a Special Adviser to the House of Commons Treasury and Civil Service Select Committee. He is a co-founder and co-editor of the magazine *Business Studies* (launched in 1988).

Professor Burton has written numerous journal articles, and his books and monographs include *Wage Inflation* (1972); *The Job-Support Machine* (1979); (with J.T. Addison) *Trade Unions and Society* (1983); *Would Workfare Work?* (1987); and *Retail Rents: Fair and Free Market?* (1992).

For the IEA he has also written extensively, including (with J.M. Buchanan and R.E. Wagner) *The Consequences of Mr Keynes* (Hobart Paper 78, 1978); 'Externalities, Property Rights, and Public Policy', in S.N.S. Cheung *et al.*, *The Myth of Social Cost* (Hobart Paper 82, 1978); *Picking Losers...?* (Hobart Paper 99, 1983); *Why No Cuts?* (Hobart Paper 104, 1985); and he edited and contributed to both N. Barry *et al.*, *Hayek's 'Serfdom' Revisited* (Hobart Paperback 18, 1984) and J. Burton *et al.*, *Keynes's General Theory: Fifty Years On* (Hobart Paperback 24, 1986).

ACKNOWLEDGEMENTS

Sunday trading regulation is a complicated, not to say arcane, area of law and particularly so in the UK. As the bulk of my research and teaching interests lie elsewhere, I could not have hoped to keep abreast of these issues over recent years but for the occasional bit of friendly advice by others far more deeply involved in Sunday trading matters than myself. In particular, I would like to thank David Ramsden, Roger Boaden and Andrew Currie of the Shopping Hours Reform Council; Malcolm Hurleston and Suzie Hughes of Hurleston Corporate Consultancy; Tony Askham of Hepherd, Winstanley and Pugh; Tony Ginty of Marks and Spencer/Retailers for Shops Act Reform; and Robert Laslett of London Economics.

The author would additionally like to thank Professor Colin Robinson and Michael Solly for their tremendous editorial work in bringing this *Hobart Paper* into publication in such a short time-span, but with such high quality.

All errors in this *Paper*, and indeed the tenor of the line of argument and of the conclusion, remain the sole responsibility of the author. My conclusions are indeed different from those for which some of the above have been campaigning.

November 1993   J.B.

This *Hobart Paper* is dedicated to the memory of my Mother and Father. As ambulance nurse and officer, respectively, there were for them no strings attached to Sunday working.

I. INTRODUCTION

Government regulation of Sunday trading has a long history in Britain, dating back at least to the Middle Ages.[1] This type of government regulation of voluntary market exchange has not always sat well with British proclivities. During the reign of Henry VI in the 15th century:

> '...the law [on Sunday trading] was frequently disregarded, since Sunday was a convenient day for those who worked during the rest of the week.'[2]

More recently, Sunday trading regulations were held to have 'lapsed' by the 1930s in Scotland, under the Scottish legal doctrine of desuetude. In the UK Sunday trading regulations formally remain today only in England and Wales. In Scotland, there has now been at least 60 years of (almost completely) deregulated Sunday trading.[3]

Sunday trading regulation remains on the Statute book in England and Wales in the form of Part IV of the Shops Act 1950. This set of regulations has had a troubled history. Indeed, there have been some 22 Bills before Parliament since 1950 seeking to reform or repeal the law. More pertinently, both supporters and critics of Sunday trading regulation would not deny that there is widespread disregard of these laws in England and Wales today.

In November 1992 the Home Secretary announced that the reform of Sunday trading would be decided by a free vote in the House of Commons on three regulatory options: total deregulation as in Scotland, a partial deregulation package as proposed by the Shopping Hours Reform Council, and a somewhat restrictionist reform proposal favoured by the Keep Sunday Special Campaign. The Draft Bill on this issue, presented in July 1993, however, lists four options for MPs to vote upon – the three aforesaid options plus another package

---

1   It has been contended that an Act regulating Sunday trading was implemented as early as the reign of King Athelstan (AD 925-941): see C. Townsend and M. Schluter, *Why Keep Sunday Special?*, Cambridge: Jubilee Centre Publications, 1985, p.7.

2   M. Harrison, *People and Shopping: A Social Background*, London: Ernest Benn, 1975, p.11.

3   Barbers and hairdressers are still prohibited by law in Scotland from doing business on Sundays.

of proposals put forward by the Retailers for Shops Act Reform Group.[4]

Synopsis of Structure and Contents

It is impossible to understand the present debate about the regulation of Sunday trading in the UK without examining the long legal and historical contexts from which the present impulse to reform has sprung and, in particular, the divergent experiences since the 1930s of England and Wales on the one hand and (deregulated) Scotland on the other. These matters are reviewed in Section II.

Section III outlines the alternative options for reform, drawing upon European and American experience, before focussing on the four specific options for reform contained in the July 1993 White Paper. The section also provides some context and clarification for these options.

We then turn to the four options in some detail. Section IV sets out the two pro-regulatory approaches to reform contained in the Draft Bill, and critically evaluates them. Section V examines the case for full and partial deregulation, whilst Section VI analyses some commonly voiced concerns about these approaches in terms of their economic and social effects. Section VII concludes with relevant issues of political economy and public choice.

Any examination of regulation and deregulation inevitably entails discussion of regulatory detail and economic technicalities. It is, however, easy to become enmeshed in the details, and to miss the wood for the trees. Lurking behind major disagreements about regulation of commercial activity there are usually deep-seated divisions of opinion, often intertwined with covert but powerful conflicts of group interest, for example, consumers *vs.* (some) producers, or one business coalition *vs.* another.

The debate about Sunday trading regulation is an example of these general points. At base, there is a fundamental schism. On the one hand are those who believe a stable and acceptable order in social and economic life must be engineered and maintained by deliberate and forceful positive actions by the state (in this instance, to maintain a 'traditional' Sunday, and the family and religious values

---

4   *Reforming the Law on Sunday Trading: A Guide to the Options for Reform,* Cm. 2300, London: HMSO, July 1993, Annex A.

hopefully associated therewith). And, on the other, are those who view culture and evolving tradition in a free society as resulting from the innumerable voluntary choices of myriads of individuals, producing a pattern of social behaviour that is orderly (but not in any way the product of governmental edict or regulatory intent).[5] Moreover, as with other debates about regulation, these disagreements over principle and perspective are interlaced with well-cloaked conflicts involving group economic interests. Regulatory schemes in business, and proposals for new, 'enhanced' regulation, are commonly – as the late Nobel Laureate George Stigler observed[6] – the product of vested interest. As we shall see, the regulation of Sunday trading in England and Wales in the 20th century seems consistent with the Stiglerian rule.

Economic analysis can help elucidate these tortuous and entangled matters. This *Paper* tries to do so, drawing upon standard price theory, the economics of time and the household, Austrian and evolutionary economics, public choice theory and the economics of regulation, business strategy analysis, the economics-and-law tradition, and, of course, relevant empirical and econometric studies.

A Personal Note

No amount of economic analysis (nor any sort of analysis – including the theological) can provide a conclusive proof of what is socially (or Divinely) right. One must at the end of the day weigh the arguments from a personal perspective. My conclusion, as with the Auld Committee in 1984,[7] is that there is – and remains – an overwhelming case for the deregulation of Sunday trading in England and Wales, in line with Scotland (and Ireland).[8]

---

5   These two concepts of order are discussed in F.A. Hayek, *Law, Legislation and Liberty*, Vol.I: *Rules and Order*, London: Kegan Paul, 1973, Ch.2.

6   G.J. Stigler, 'The Theory of Economic Regulation', *Bell Journal of Economics*, Vol.2, No.1, 1971.

7   *The Shops Acts: Late Night and Sunday Opening*, Cmnd. 9376, London: HMSO, November 1984 (referred to hereinafter as The Auld Report/Committee of Inquiry, after its chairman).

8   Northern Ireland is not mentioned in the Government's draft Bill on Sunday trading reform. The implicit intention is that this region will retain its existing Sunday trading regulations despite the move to reform in England and Wales, and the fully deregulated status of Sunday trading in the Irish Republic and Scotland.

II. THE LEGAL AND HISTORICAL BACKGROUND

The present framework of Sunday trading regulation in England and Wales is contained in the Shops Act 1950 (in particular, Part IV of the Act), a consolidating measure which drew on and incorporated previous Acts and Regulations from 1912 to 1938. But there was a long history of prior Sunday trading legislation in the UK.

A Potted History of UK Sunday Trading Regulation

In 1448, Henry VI prohibited the conduct of fairs and markets on Sundays and the sale of goods in churchyards on that day. There has been some movement since then, as many Church of England (and Roman Catholic) churches nowadays contain stalls and shops purveying various articles on Sundays!

The Sunday Observance Act of 1677 prohibited many activities on Sundays (including the undertaking of sports). This legislation survived for almost three centuries, even though it was much ignored, before being repealed in 1969. The Auld Committee noted in its 1984 report that '...long before this century it had become hopelessly inadequate as a means of enforcement'.[9] In the late 19th century, however, several attempts were made to impose other, new restrictions on Sunday trading – which were not received with much public approval. Indeed, the Sunday Trading Bill put forward by Lord Robert Grosvenor in 1855 led to a riot of 150,000 protestors in Hyde Park and the showering of the Prime Minister's coach with a rain of fruit and stones. The Bill was withdrawn.

In 1936 two Acts were passed as a result of Private Members Bills, The Shops (Sunday Trading Restriction) Act 1936, and The Retail Meat Dealers' Shops (Sunday Closing) Act 1936. Their promoters justified these measures – which applied to England and Wales only, not Scotland – in terms of lofty objectives such as the protection of the interests of small traders, the provision of a day of rest for shopworkers, and the maintenance of the 'traditional' character of a Sunday.

---

9   Auld Committee, *op. cit.*, p.2.

There was, however, a somewhat less lofty foundation. The Private Members' Bills that preceded the Acts were promoted by organised coalitions of businesses – for example, in the case of the Shops (Sunday Trading Restrictions) Act 1936 by the mill-owners and the Early Closing Association; and in the case of the Retail Meat Dealers' Shops (Sunday Closing) Act by the National Federation of Meat Traders.[10] A possible interpretation of these legislative measures, then, is that they were anti-competitive devices vigorously sponsored by organised producer interest groups, to the detriment of the (unorganised) consumer interest. Patient historical research would be necessary to try to discern the true balance of motives lurking behind these two Acts: the avowed intentions on the one hand, and the attempt to restrict competition via activity in the political market on the other. When producer coalitions seek to still the winds of competition, they very commonly cloak their motives in the rhetoric of the 'public interest'.

After the Second World War, a Departmental Committee (the Gowers Committee) was appointed to assess whether the existing Shops Acts should be reformed or amended. Their report found, amongst other things, that '...in certain respects the law is neither observed nor enforceable, and has been brought into contempt'.[11]

The Shops Act 1950: Origins

The Gowers Committee made detailed recommendations for simplifying and rationalising the existing Sunday trading restrictions, which they found neither simple nor intelligible. The Government reaction was to pass the Shops Act 1950 as a temporary, stop-gap measure of consolidation. Whilst this 'temporary' measure did present Sunday trading restrictions in England and Wales in perhaps a somewhat more

---

10 The 'Early Closing Association' was a complex producer lobby composed of the National Chamber of Trade, the Drapers Chamber of Trade, the National Federation of Grocers and two trade unions – the National Union of Shopworkers and the National Union of Distributive Workers. The earlier Hairdressers and Barbers (Sunday Closing) Act 1930 was also the result of political pressure from these trades.

11 *Closing Hours of Shops* (the Gowers Report), Cmnd. 7105, London: HMSO, April 1947.

convenient form than previously, the 1984 Auld Committee of Inquiry found that

'...it did nothing to cure the obscurity, the anomalies, and the problems of enforcement identified in the [Gowers] Report'.[12]

The Shops Act 1950, based as it was on 1936 and earlier Acts (which had themselves proved inadequate and unenforceable), was out of date *even in the very year of its passage through Parliament.* This, however, with very minor modifications,[13] remains the law at the time of writing. Some 40 plus years later, and after more than 20 attempts to reform it in Parliament over that period, this 'temporary measure' is still with us in 1993.

Few – including leading members of the Keep Sunday Special Campaign – would now deny that there is an unanswerable general case for the reform of English and Welsh Sunday trading restrictions, to bring the legislative environment of retailing in this respect into line with modern conditions. The argument is over what the nature of the reforms should be.

The Shops Act 1950: Contents

The Act deals with matters such as general closing hours, early closing and conditions of employment (for example, for young persons). It is Part IV of the Act which deals with Sunday trading in England and Wales.[14] Section 47 of the Act stipulates that 'Every shop shall... be closed for the serving of customers on Sundays [in England and Wales]'.

Working in shops (for example, stacking, cleaning, deliveries, display arrangement) is not illegal on Sundays; it is *serving customers* (except in Scotland) which constitutes a crime. The Act, however, makes shopkeepers, not shoppers,

---

12 Auld, *op. cit.*, p.3.

13 For instance, the West Midlands County Council Act 1980 exempted the National Exhibition Centre, Birmingham, from the Shops Act restrictions on Sunday trading during the course of an exhibition.

14 Sections 22 and 23 of Part II of the Act also deal, however, with Sunday employment. For example, Section 22 stipulates that any person employed in a shop for more than four hours on a Sunday must be provided with a whole-day holiday on some other day, and must not be employed for more than two other Sundays in the same month. It would be possible to repeal Section IV whilst retaining these Part II restrictions.

subject to criminal penalties for breach of Sunday trading restrictions; currently the maximum fine is £2,500, and it is District and Borough Councils (not the police) which are the enforcement and prosecuting bodies for the Shops Act 1950.[15]

The general provision against Sunday opening in England and Wales contained in the quotation from Section 47 of the Act would superficially seem as clear as clear can be. But this is not so, because *within the same Section* the Act goes on to say that shops may indeed open in England and Wales to serve customers ... provided that the transactions involved are covered in the Fifth Schedule of the Act which contains a list of items which *can* be sold on Sunday in England and Wales. The contents of this Fifth Schedule have been the source of much objection to the Sunday trading rules, and we shall return to the matter below.

The Act also makes provision for those who observe the Jewish Sabbath to close on Saturdays whilst opening on Sundays. No such special provision is made in the Act, however, for followers of the Moslem faith (or, indeed, for any other religious or ethnic group, let alone agnostics and atheists). The framers of Sunday trading rules in 1936 and 1950 could not, of course, have foreseen the commitment to a multicultural society which now exists.

The Act also allows other exceptions to the 'general' provision against Sunday opening. Local authorities in areas with 'holiday resorts' within their borders are given the discretion (under Section 51) to allow certain classes of shop to open on Sundays (for not more than 18 Sundays in any one year) to purvey items covered in the Seventh Schedule of the Act (such as photographic requisites, postcards, and articles 'required for the purposes of bathing or fishing').[16] Local authorities may also (under Section 48) make a 'Partial Exemption Order' allowing for the serving of customers in shops before 10.00 a.m. on Sundays of certain items listed in

---

15 Local authorities also have the right to ask for a civil remedy for breach of the Shops Act, by applying for an injunction from the High Court. This has the effect of causing shops to close on Sundays.

16 But not, by omission, articles relating to running, bird-watching, skating or golf, etc. However, the Fifth Schedule does allow for the sale on Sunday of sports requisites provided they are sold at the premises where sports are conducted. Such contortions underline the general complexity of the Act and its Schedules.

the Sixth Schedule of the Act, which include 'fancy bread', groceries, and fish. Somewhat curiously, however, the Act made it unlawful for fish and chip shops to trade on Sundays.

It is widely recognised that Section IV of the Shops Act 1950 suffers from anomalies and a related problem of enforcement.

The Problem of Anomalies

The items exempted from the general proscription of Sunday trading in England and Wales under the Fifth Schedule make interesting, if curious, reading to the contemporary observer. For example, it permits the sale of 'fresh or partly cooked tripe', and 'fodder for horses... at any farm... or inn'.

There is, in short, an apparent time-warp in this list as it applies to contemporary behaviour on Sundays. This is not at all surprising since the exemptions were all drawn from pre-1950 legislation (as described above), some of it pre-First World War vintage! The inadequacies of this out-of-date list had indeed drawn scathing judicial comment in the late 1930s, let alone more recent times.

Nevertheless, the law is the law. The result is a most curious pattern of items that are lawfully-tradeable and non-lawfully-tradeable on Sunday in England and Wales. Amongst the many notorious contrasts are that it is lawful for an English shop to sell a bulb for your car headlight but not for a light in your WC! Again, it is quite lawful for cinemas to show a film on a Sunday, but a shop cannot hire out this same film on video to someone who wants to view it at home.[17] A longer list of the anomalies embedded in the 1950 Act is provided in Box A.

In short, the Act abounds with inconsistencies. It is difficult to believe that any coherent set of 'objectives' is served by the items listed in the Fifth Schedule.

The Problem of Enforcement

Inconsistency inevitably leads to enforcement difficulties, as both shoppers and shopkeepers are unaware of the

---

17 Videos obviously did not exist in 1950, and therefore could not be listed in Schedule 5 of the Act. This points to the general problem that all such lists of exemptions must become outmoded over time in innovative economies experiencing the almost-continuous introduction of new products and services.

Shops Act 1950

Examples of items that can and cannot be sold legally in England and Wales on Sundays:

Legal		Illegal
Ice Cream	*not*	Fish Fingers
Fresh Milk	*not*	Dried Milk
Newspapers	*not*	Toilet Paper
Car Battery	*not*	Torch Battery
Car Fuse	*not*	House Fuse
Fan Belt	*not*	Tights
Gin	*not*	Baby's Bottle
Cigarettes	*not*	Fresh Meats
Fresh Fruit	*not*	Tinned Fruit
Freshly Cooked Bacon	*not*	Pre-packed Bacon
Bottled Water	*not*	Fruit Juice
Fresh Cream	*not*	Evaporated Milk
Cigarette Lighters	*not*	Fire Lighters
Fresh Vegetables	*not*	Frozen Vegetables
Mars Bars	*not*	Digestive Biscuits
Car Oil	*not*	Cooking Oil

Source: Shopping Hours Reform Council

complexities involved; indeed, 'the statute is a complicated piece of legislation, not easy [even] for a lawyer to understand and interpret'.[18]

---

18 Auld, *op. cit.*, p.5.

To add to this confusing situation, there have been major variations in local authority enforcement policies, both in the vigour of prosecution and the type of shop prosecuted. For example, Camden Council in London has evidently followed for many years a *laissez-faire* policy of condoning very extensive shop and street trading on Sundays around its High Street and Camden Lock. Others launch selective prosecutions, commonly responding to complaints of breach brought to them.[19] Over the past few years typically only a couple of hundred cases have come before the courts in any year, and typically also against a small number of large retail chains.

To summarise, the present Sunday trading regulations in England and Wales are patchily enforced, widely disregarded, and commonly not understood by shoppers and small shop-keepers alike.

The Failure of Reform Initiatives

The supposedly 'temporary' nature of the Shops Act 1950, its perceived anachronisms, and the problems of enforcement it entails might suggest that it is an area of government regulation ripe for reform. As noted above, there have been over 20 attempts mounted in Parliament since 1950 so to do. None succeeded. Why has that been so?

The lessons are encapsulated in the failure of the Shops Bill introduced by Mrs Thatcher's Government in 1985. This followed the Report of the Auld Committee of Inquiry of 1984 which strongly argued the case that all remaining legal controls on the opening hours of shops should be abolished. When the Report was debated in the Commons initially, its recommendations obtained a majority of 120 in favour. But in April 1986 the Bill fell at Second Reading by 14 votes following a Conservative backbench rebellion, although it had successfully gone through the House of Lords.

Parliament was lobbied hard not only by Churches and the Keep Sunday Special Campaign, but also by a motley of vested producer interests including various retailers/retail coalitions with interests against reform and, most vociferously, by the trade union USDAW (representing then about 12 per cent of the total retail workforce in the UK). USDAW, in partnership

---

19 It is not unknown for shops to use this tactic to 'make trouble' for their competitors.

with the Co-operative Movement, has opposed longer trading hours for shops in the past, and between them they were a powerful influence behind the parliamentary fight against Sunday trading reforming legislation whenever it was introduced. Other unions with shopworker members have also long opposed extensions of trading hours (even though there is no necessary connection between hours of trading and hours of work).

Retailers and trade unions obviously have legitimate interests in these matters. The facts would suggest, however, that this concentrated lobbying power may have had an influence on the policy reform process out of proportion to the much larger, but much more dispersed, consumer interest in Sunday trading reform. It seems no exaggeration to conclude that the impulse to reform over some four decades has been stymied by, in particular, the disproportionate influence of producer interest groups on the political process.

Further Complexities Resulting from EC Law

Towards the end of the 1980s the question was raised in British courts whether Section 47 of the Shops Act 1950, quite apart from the domestic difficulties associated with it, additionally fell foul of Article 30 of the 1957 Treaty of Rome, which provides that

> 'Quantitative restrictions on imports, and all measures having equivalent effect shall ... be prohibited between the Member States'.

The argument here was that the Sunday trading restrictions in England and Wales reduced the market for certain goods exported to the UK (such as Dutch bulbs and Italian bathrooms retailed by DIY chains), and thus breached Article 30. The matter was referred to the European Court of Justice (ECJ), which initially produced a somewhat opaque judgement in respect of *Torfaen Borough Council v B & Q plc* ([1990] 1 CMLR 337), but which gave some foundation to this contention.

There followed a number of years of 'buckpassing' from national courts and the House of Lords of matters for decision to the ECJ, and what appears to be a case of 'moving the goalposts' on the part of the latter. The ECJ had originally

[21]

ruled in commenting on the aforementioned *Torfaen* case that such restrictions were potentially compatible with Community law provided that 'the restrictive effects on Community trade which may result therefrom do not exceed the effects intrinsic to rules of that kind'. This has been called the 'proportionality test'. The ECJ also laid down that it was for the national courts to assess whether this test was passed by a domestic restriction 'as a question of fact'.

By the nature of things, courts in England and Wales (as elsewhere) are not experienced in estimating trade flows. Nor did the ECJ provide instruction on how to determine these matters and how then to perform a balancing judgement on the 'effects intrinsic to rules of that kind'. The stage was set for considerable confusion, with different English and Welsh courts arriving at different judgements.

Whilst the British courts were struggling with these issues, however, there were two more ECJ rulings on Sunday trading in respect of French and Belgian laws that restricted the employment of employees on Sundays.[20] In these cases, the ECJ made up its own mind and simply jumped to the conclusion that the restrictive effects on trade were *not* disproportionate to the presumed aim pursued (the protection of shopworkers). However:

> 'In neither case did the Court explain why it had decided to perform a task which, in *Torfaen*, it expressly said was the responsibility of the national courts.'[21]

Proceedings referred to the ECJ by the House of Lords seemed to produce a further change of mind, in the Court's rulings on *Stoke-on-Trent City Council v B & Q plc* ([1993] 1 CMLR 426). In this decision it abandoned entirely the position it had taken in *Torfaen* and announced that 'Article 30 ... does not apply to national legislation prohibiting retailers from opening their premises on Sunday'. In short, there is no need for a 'proportionality' test at all.

These decisions of the ECJ are unsatisfactory in a number of ways. First, they are *prima facie* inconsistent. Second, the ECJ failed to explain why it is that such legislation is not caught by

---

20 *Union Departmentale des Syndicats de l'Aisne v Conforma* (1991) 1 ECR 997, and *Ministere Publique v Marchandise* [1991], 1 ECR 1027.

21 A. Arnull, 'Anyone for Tripe?', University of Birmingham: Faculty of Law (mimeo), 1993.

Article 30. Third, it is disputable that Part IV of the Shops Act 1950 has the same objectives as the French and Belgian laws restricting the employment of workers on Sundays. It is *other* Parts of the Shops Act that deal with conditions of employment and the protection of shopworkers, and not Part IV. Moreover, as we have earlier seen, the 'objectives' of the entire Act are obscure – the Preamble states only that it is an Act of consolidation – and those relating to Part IV in particular do not seem to have any sustainable rationale.

The results of the most recent ECJ decision are of *increasing incongruence* with the domestic UK Sunday trading scene, in two ways. *First*, in the run-up to Christmas 1991 many major supermarket chains – Tesco, Asda, Gateway, Safeway and (more reluctantly) Sainsbury – openly 'defied the law in England and Wales by trading on a Sunday for the first time'.[22] A similar pattern of events obtained in the pre-Christmas 1992 period. At the same time, supermarket shopping on Sundays increased, with the market research firm Nielson finding in late 1991 that more than 1 million households in England and Wales were engaged in supermarket grocery shopping on Sundays.[23] *Second*, faced with widespread flouting and disregard of Sunday trading laws (despite ECJ rulings which appear to support such restrictions), the British Government was impelled to act. The 1992 Conservative Manifesto gave a clear commitment to the reform of the Sunday trading laws (once the outcome of the *Stoke-on-Trent* case, then before the ECJ, was known). These are the origins of the White Paper published in July 1993. In the next section we turn to a consideration of its proposals.

Sunday Trading in England and Wales on the Eve of Reform

The situation today is that there has been a substantial move in the direction of the progressive abandonment of Sunday trading restrictions by a combination of private action and governmental inaction. As the Auld Inquiry revealed, these restrictions were widely ignored and in practice increasingly unenforceable some 10 years ago. The opening of major chains of supermarkets on Sundays in the 1990s has aggravated the problem.

---

22 'Christmas Present for Law-Breakers', *Guardian*, 30 November 1991, p.6.

23 P. Wintour and D. McKie, 'Noon Start for Sunday Shops Plan', *Sunday Times*, 11 December 1991, p.7.

Until the ruling of the ECJ reported in January 1993 regarding the *Stoke-on-Trent* case, retailers in England and Wales could claim, as has Safeway, that

> 'The UK law remains confused and unclear. We will continue to accede to the clear and growing demand of our customers to shop on Sundays.'[24]

But the ECJ ruling in *Stoke-on-Trent* – whatever its deficiencies – meant that the previous opaque *Torfaen* decision was abandoned, and that local authorities were indeed 'entitled to seek an injunction preventing Sunday opening by offending retailers'.[25] This, however, is not entirely an end to the European Law dimensions of this long and tortuous wrangle, in that the Shops Act 1950 has been challenged in the courts on the grounds of alleged incompatibility with the Equal Treatment Directive (Directive 76/207), as in *Chisholm v Kirklees Metropolitan Borough Council* (1993).[26] This latest challenge will doubtless have to go to the ECJ for final clarification and (typically) take another two years to be resolved, unless it is sidestepped by the Government (as it now intends) bringing in legislation to reform the 1950 Act.

Meanwhile, many local authorities have declined to prosecute retailers opening on Sundays in England and Wales, despite the ECJ opening of this door. For example, in December 1992, Westminster City Council said that '...it would turn a blind eye to [Sunday] trading'.[27] In this more relaxed atmosphere, the well-known department store, Selfridges, decided to open for Sunday business for the first time in its 80-year history.

Not all major retailers have gone down this path. In particular, Marks & Spencer, the UK's leading high street retailer, refused to follow this course of action, and printed no less than 10 million leaflets (deposited in all customers'

24 F. Gibb, D. Broom and T. Walker, 'Judge Opens Door to Prosecution of Sunday Traders', *The Times*, 9 July 1993, p.2.

25 'Sunday Trading – Again', *European Law Monitor*, Vol.1, Issue 5, June 1993, p.9.

26 As reported in R. Rice, 'Sunday Ban "Discriminatory"', *The Times*, 22 May 1993, p.10.

27 H. Smith, 'Sunday Trading to Go Ahead', *Evening Standard*, 17 December 1992, p.17.

carrier bags by their check-out operators) to announce that 'as a matter of principle Marks & Spencer will remain closed on Sundays'.[28] M & S is a leading supporter of the lobby which has recently emerged calling itself 'The Retailers for Shops Act Reform' Group (RSAR). This lobby supports a restrictionist reform of the law along somewhat similar lines to those advocated by the Keep Sunday Special Campaign (KSSC: see Sections III and IV).

It is, in short, apparent that there is currently a division of strategy about the future reform of Sunday trading in England and Wales as between different major retailing chains. Some advocate partial deregulation, whilst others favour a more restrictionist régime.

Students of political economy might care to reflect on the following points. First, the at times raucous debate on the reform of Sunday trading continues to be dominated today, as in earlier decades, by powerful and organised coalitions of producers with very direct business strategy interests in the outcome of reform. There is also an ostensibly religion-based campaign (Keep Sunday Special) which, however, may well have considerable support from some important retail groups (including John Lewis, Austin Reed, Threshers, the Co-op, and Fortnum & Mason).

Second, the power and influence of these organised lobbies may be appreciated from the fact that three of the four options for change on Sunday trading presented to Parliament in the July 1993 White Paper are the very sets of proposals favoured by these self-same organised lobbies. Only the option of full deregulation of Sunday trading in England and Wales, on the lines of the Scottish model, has no organised lobby to support it.[29] One purpose of this *Hobart*

---

28 See report in G. Bowditch, 'M&S Deliver Sunday Message', *The Times*, 3 December 1992, p.21. M&S do, however, open some of their stores on Sundays throughout the year in Scotland.

29 The Prime Minister, Mr John Major, has expressed his personal view that the present Sunday trading laws in England and Wales are 'bizarre', and the hope that eventual reform would follow the Scottish model (in reply to Prime Minister's Questions in the House of Commons in December 1990). On 26 November 1992, however, the Home Secretary announced that the choice between options by MPs would not be subject to a Government Whip (except for the issue of shopworkers' rights not to work on Sundays). The Government, in short, will not back the opportunity for full deregulation – as it did with the Shops Bill 1985 – with its own marshalled Parliamentary support.

Paper is to examine the economic and related philosophical arguments in favour of full deregulation.

Conclusions on the Legal and Political Background

Laws on Sunday trading have a long, complicated history in Britain. Over the past 40 years there has been widespread evasion of these regulations in England and Wales, clearly reaching new heights (or depths) within the last few years.

Over the same four decades, numerous attempts to reform this chaotic regulatory situation have been held in a gridlock by various political forces but most importantly by the clash of organised sectional interests. This disproportionate influence of interest groups in the matter (particularly producer groups) threatens to dominate the discussion of, and MPs' decisions about, the options for change now placed before Parliament.

The general confusion over Sunday trading issues in England and Wales has also been marked in recent years by complexities arising from the interface between national regulations and EC law.[30] The clarification of this matter by the ECJ (even if its decisions appear highly questionable) finally pushed the British political system to the point where a reform of Sunday trading laws had perforce to be undertaken.

With these points in mind, we turn in Section III to an elaboration of, and some commentary upon, the alternative proposals for reform contained in the Government's White Paper of July 1993.

---

[30] Students interested in examining further some of the complex issues of law and law-and-economics that have been involved might wish to consult I.P.H. Diamond, 'The Shops Act and the EEC Treaty', *Justice of the Peace*, 28 January 1989, pp.51-55; P. Diamond, 'Dishonourable Defences: The Use of Injunctions and the EEC Treaty – Case Study of the Shops Act 1950', *Modern Law Review*, Vol.54, No.1, January 1991, pp.72-87; and A.J. Askham, T. Burke and D. Ramsden, *EC Sunday Trading*, London: Butterworths, 1990, Ch. 18 on 'The Economic Issue' in particular.

III. WHAT OPTIONS FOR REFORM?

Before turning to the details of the four options for the reform of Sunday trading in England and Wales selected by the Government, it is valuable to remind ourselves of the wide variety of models adopted elsewhere.

The European Patchwork on Sunday Trading

It is not necessary to venture outside Western Europe to observe a large medley of different Sunday trading regulatory régimes. They include:

o Countries with no Sunday trading regulations at all – the 'deregulation' option of the Government's Draft Bill (Republic of Ireland, Scotland and Sweden);

o Countries with a general ban against the employment of retail workers on Sundays but with wide exemptions for particular kinds of shops (for example, Belgium);

o Stringent prohibition of Sunday trading with only limited exemptions (the German model);

o A system in which the right of shops to trade on Sundays is effectively entrenched in constitutional law (Spain);[31]

o A 'schizoid' system which combines the principle of a commercial right for shops to trade throughout the entire week (without legal restraint on opening hours) with a general prohibition against the employment of salaried shopworkers on Sundays (the French case);[32]

---

31 This differs from the Irish-Scottish-Swedish model in that in this group of countries there is only an *absence* of statutory regulation of Sunday trading, and this state does not flow as a *right* from constitutional guarantees relating to freedom of enterprise (as in Spain).

32 This seemingly paradoxical legal situation is ameliorated by a good dose of pragmatic exemption. All family and self-employed retail businesses fall outside the prohibition against Sunday employment; there are considerable exemptions in respect of certain kinds of shops; exemptions may also be obtained at the discretion of the local mayor. In practice this ends up as a system with wide regional variations.

o The local authority autonomy model, whereby regulatory decisions upon opening hours are devolved entirely from central to local government (as in Portugal).[33] In practice this has resulted not in wide local variations but rather an effectively deregulated system of Sunday trading with some limited regional variations.

There is, in short, no common or even 'central tendency' model of Sunday trading regulation in Western Europe. Moreover, there are considerable variations in popular compliance with, and public enforcement of, such Sunday trading restrictions as exist among European countries (and indeed from region to region in certain countries, notably Belgium and Greece).

Pressure for greater liberalisation is emerging generally, both at the domestic and European levels (as exemplified by the formation of the shopping hours liberalisation lobby 'Euroshop' in Brussels in 1992).

...And the American Patchwork

The United States reveals equally wide variations in Sunday trading regulatory models, these laws being a matter of state (not federal) decision and jurisdiction.

Historically the United States was the paradigm of extremely restrictionist Sunday trading prohibition, under the 'Blue Laws' first enacted in that country's colonial period.[34] From the late 19th century onwards, however, pressures for reform or repeal of these laws appeared from a variety of political quarters, including those (such as Jewish merchants) who argued that the Blue Laws infringed their constitutional rights.[35] From the 1960s onwards a move towards deregulation/liberalisation became manifest. Whereas in

---

[33] Local governments in Portugal have the regulatory power over opening/closing hours in regard to all 7 days of the week, within the nationally prescribed limits of maximum opening from 6 a.m. to midnight.

[34] The Blue Laws were named after the colour of the paper on which they were printed in the colonial era, and owe their origin to the Old Testament inclinations of the original Puritan colonists of the Eastern seaboard of America.

[35] J.A. Barron, 'Sunday in North America', *Harvard Law Review*, Vol.79, November 1965, pp.42-54.

1970 there were some 25 states with state-wide Blue Laws (albeit enforced with varying degrees of zeal), by 1984 this total had fallen to 13.[36]

Summarising the current situation in the United States is difficult, given the considerable diversity of the country and the continuation of regulatory change at the state level. One estimate is that by the end of the 1980s, only five states retained substantial or total restrictions on Sunday opening, whilst in nine states the regulatory system had dissolved into a fragmentary patchwork of local options, the (predominant) remainder having only minor or no restrictions.[37]

The Restricted British Menu for Reform

The Government's Draft Bill on the reform of Sunday trading law in England and Wales limits the parliamentary choice among alternative régimes to but four options, three of which have arisen from the proposals of organised British lobby groups: the Keep Sunday Special Campaign (KSSC); the Shopping Hours Reform Council (SHRC); and the Retailers for Shops Act Reform (RSAR). As the foregoing synopses of the many European and American models make clear, these four options are a small sample of the many alternatives that could in principle have been put before Parliament for consideration.

Obviously, practical considerations dictate that Parliament cannot debate and decide between a myriad alternatives for reform. Nevertheless, there is a particular *lacuna* in the restricted package of alternatives on offer which is lamentable from the perspective of public choice analysis.

The Missing Option

A reform option omitted from the Bill is based on the principle of local government discretion (as in Portugal and a number of American states). Such a system has a number of attractions: citizens can use their votes in the local political market to influence local authority regulation, and they can

---

36 Association of General Merchandising Chains, Inc., *Summary of State Laws Which Restrict Retail Business on Sunday*, Washington DC, 1984.

37 T. Burke and J.R. Shackleton, *Sunday, Sunday: The Issues in Sunday Trading*, London: Adam Smith Institute, 1989, Table II, p.28.

also 'vote with their feet' residentially if they find the ambience of local government decision-making unattractive.[38] There is indeed evidence to support the thesis that people with similar tastes for public goods tend to live in the same locality.[39] Shopping (including Sunday shopping) is a largely local activity, generating local benefits (economic activity) and imposing some local 'public bads' (such as noise, traffic). There is an obvious case for allowing local preferences to predominate in the formation of the relevant regulatory framework.

The Auld Committee in 1984 accepted that there were attractions to a system of local government discretion on Sunday trading matters, but rejected any such reform on the grounds that the result would be 'a lack of consistency... both geographically and over time'. In its view, this would 'aggravate the variations that the present inconsistent enforcement of the law has produced'.[40]

What this conclusion blithely ignored was the existence of a *process of regulatory competition* between competing jurisdictions. The possibility of retail businesses and residents-council taxpayers voting with their feet would put economic restraints on capricious decisions by local authorities. The evidence from Portugal supports this contention. There, the system of local authority autonomy on Sunday trading regulation has not resulted in a chaos of inconsistent regulatory patterns (as feared by Auld), but rather a general pattern of seven days a week opening with some local and circumscribed departures from this norm.

When, rather late in the day, the Government took up the idea of putting a fourth option before Parliament in addition to the three originally announced in November 1992 (full deregulation, and the KSSC and SHRC options) it thus missed a golden opportunity to proffer a genuinely alternatively-based approach of local authority determination for parliamentary consideration. The RSAR option which was

---

38 The original economic analysis of the public choice outcome (in respect of public goods provision and residential choice) in a system of autonomous local governments is contained in C.M. Tiebout, 'A Pure Theory of Local Expenditures', *Journal of Political Economy*, Vol.LXIV, October 1956, pp.416-24.

39 See R.L. Bish, *The Public Economy of Metropolitan Areas*, Chicago: Markham, 1971.

40 Auld, *op. cit.*, paras. 226-227.

in fact selected as the fourth runner is, as we shall see below, only slightly removed from the KSSC approach.

Readers may consider this discussion as somewhat 'academic' in that it is the RSAR option which is on the agenda, and a local authority-based system is not – so, why bother to discuss the latter? On the contrary, however, this points to a central deficiency in the whole process of regulatory reform through the political process.

The RSAR option jumped onto the agenda late in the day because it was backed by a well-organised lobby that had suddenly emerged amongst a group of producers. The option of a system of local authority determination – which on economic and public choice grounds has a number of features to recommend it – had no such vocal and powerfully-backed lobby. The first reached the reform agenda; the second did not. A persistent danger of both regulation-making and reform thereof is that both the agenda and the content of regulation are subject to hijacking by organised producer interests.

Further Caveats About the Draft Bill Options

The Government's White Paper on the options for the reform of Sunday trading law tries to provide a definitive guide to the four models to be considered by Parliament.[41] But there are a number of qualifications which should be made to this guide.

'Fluid' Options

In describing three of the four options as 'the' KSSC, SHRC and RSAR models (as Cm. 2300 does), it should be noted that they are not the same as they were (say) three years ago – indeed, the RSAR 'model' did not even *exist* in any form until early 1993, and has been further modified since the publication of Cm. 2300 in July 1993.

There has been some (relatively small) change in the content of the SHRC proposals over the years. By contrast, the content of 'the' KSSC model has changed considerably over time. These proposals were (as described below) first presented to Parliament in the form of the Shops (Amendment) Bill of 1992, also known as 'the Powell Bill' after its chief

---

41 *Reforming the Law on Sunday Trading: A Guide to the Options for Reform*, Cm. 2300, London: HMSO, 1993, Ch.2, 'The Models for Reform'.

parliamentary sponsor, Mr Ray Powell, MP. The proposals set out in Cm. 2300 as 'the' KSSC model are by any standard a very considerable watering down of the rigours of restriction initially envisaged in the Powell Bill (and have since been further modified).

Yet the KSSC has maintained for many years that its proposals rest upon clear principles (which they term the REST Principles, also described below) which are capable of unambiguous translation into concrete policy measures on Sunday trading restriction. How does commitment to inviolable principle square with fluidity of policy proposal?

No doubt KSSC supporters could claim that in the course of discussion of the Powell Bill it became clear that certain aspects of the original proposals were impracticable. Economists will also recognise, however, that another force may well be at work – the incentive for the KSSC to protect its potential share of MPs' (and Lords') votes, subsequent to the recent entry to the array of 'permitted' policy options of the RSAR. The vote-seeking strategy is to 'move in close' to the position of the new entrant.

In terms of the economics of political competition,[42] the calculus of incentives is as follows. Given the probable spectrum of MPs' preferences on the Sunday trading issue, the KSSC position is popularly conceived as the most restrictive option on offer, with deregulation at the other extreme, and with the SHRC option somewhere in between. The RSAR model entered this competition also in between the KSSC and SHRC positions – but, as most observers would diagnose it, somewhat closer to the former than the latter. To protect its expected share of the vote from the erosion of affiliation caused by the new entrant, there is an incentive for a lobby such as the KSSC to move its announced position closer to that of the new competitor. Over the Summer of 1993 the models of both the KSSC and the RSAR were further modified from those which appeared in Cm. 2300.

---

42 The analysis which follows is a compressed verbal account of propositions in the economic analysis of multi-'party' competition, which really requires some simple diagrammatics to convey the argument fully. Students interested in these matters are referred to the classic work of A. Downs, *The Economic Theory of Democracy*, New York: Harper and Row, 1965, and the admirable, shorter introduction to this type of analysis by G. Tullock, *The Vote Motive*, Hobart Paperback No.9, London: Institute of Economic Affairs, 1976.

Deviation on Sunday Working Terms and Conditions

Integral to the original proposals of the SHRC, KSSC and RSAR on the reform of Sunday trading regulations were their own, distinctive sets of proposals regarding the creation of new employment rights for shopworkers in respect of Sunday work. For example, a key element in the original specification of the SHRC position were proposals to provide new *statutory protection* of all shopworkers in respect of:

o A newly-created statutory right for shop staff against discrimination by employers for refusing to work on Sundays;

o A new right to withdraw from Sunday work on grounds of conscience at one month's notice;

o A statutory stipulation of a standard 39-hour work-week (with hours worked in excess at agreed premium rates);

o The premium for Sunday shop work to be 'established according to the practice prevailing in each shop'.[43]

The alternative proposals of the KSSC and the RSAR vary considerably – for example, the KSSC model in original format replaced SHRC condition (d) (the fourth point above) with a new statutory requirement of double-time payment for Sunday work.

In Cm. 2300, the Government removed these variations, and replaced them by a new, *common*, set of shopworker protection proposals of its own devising. Thus 'the' SHRC, RSAR and KSSC models in the Draft Bill are, in fact, substantially altered variants of those originally formulated with regard to their proposals on shopworker Sunday employment conditions.

The Government-imposed common element to all of the four options contained in Cm. 2300 is that

'...all those employed as shopworkers in England and Wales, at the time that any changes in the law governing Sunday trading are

---

43 Condensed from 'SHRC Policy and Statutory Protection for Shopworkers', London: Shopping Hours Reform Council Briefing Notes, 1992.

brought into effect, will be specially protected against being compelled to work on Sunday if they do not wish to do so.' (Cm. 2300, para. 12)

'…The dismissal of such employees would be automatically unfair if the reason for it was a refusal to work on a Sunday.' (Cm. 2300, para. 13)

It should be emphasised that these proposed additional shopworker statutory rights apply only to *existing* staff, and not to both *existing* and *future* employees.[44] Moreover, these additional rights are proposed to apply whether or not existing shopworkers (in England and Wales, not Scotland or N. Ireland) have already signed contracts agreeing to work on Sundays.[45,46]

In taking this particular line, the Government has in effect adopted the employment rights proposal of two leading British economic advocates of the deregulation option[47] – that reform should be accompanied by the introduction of a statutory right to compensation for existing employees if dismissed for refusing to work on Sundays – and applied it across the board to all of the four options.

It has been suggested in a recent newspaper report that the Government is negotiating behind the scenes to compromise on this matter, and to concede to *all* shop employees (both existing and future) the right to opt out from Sunday working. The same report suggests that this move has been prompted by a fear that *none* of the four options, as presently stipulated, might obtain a Parliamentary majority.[48] This is not a confirmed development in Government policy, but may be informed speculation. It does, however, underline the fluidity surrounding these matters, as discussed above.

---

44 The original SHRC, KSSC and RSAR proposals envisaged statutory protection for refusal to work on Sundays for *both* categories.

45 Employers will be bound to obtain their consent in writing to a continuation of these arrangements.

46 The Draft Bill envisages no qualifying period of employment or hours of work per week requirement for these new rights to obtain.

47 T. Burke and J.R. Shackleton, *op. cit.*, Section 3.6.

48 C. Lewington and A. Law, 'Doors Open for Sunday Trading', *Sunday Express*, 7 November 1993, pp.1-2.

We now discuss the four models for modernising the regulation of Sunday trading in England and Wales set out in the Government's *Guide to the Options for Reform*.[49] Section IV examines the two regulatory approaches to reform contained therein (the KSSC and RSAR models), whilst Section V turns to the other two alternatives of full and partial deregulation.

---

[49] It is only fair to note that Cm. 2300 itself contains (Ch.2) an admirably succinct and clear summary of these proposals, as they stood before the modifications to the KSSC and RSAR models introduced subsequently. It also contains much photographic material (e.g. in relation to shop sizes and types) which gives an immediate and helpful visual impression of the implications for shop opening and closing on Sundays under the four options.

IV. REGULATORY APPROACHES TO REFORM

The two regulatory reform options outlined in Cm. 2300 are the schemes proposed respectively by the Keep Sunday Special Campaign (KSSC) and the Retailers for Shops Act Reform (RSAR). This Section explains and evaluates these schemes.[50]

1. The KSSC Model(s)

The KSSC view is based upon the premise that

> '...the current law (i.e. Part IV of the Shops Act 1950) has a coherent foundation. To a very high degree its specific provisions can be explained in terms of comprehensive principles. It is an Act which can be polished and updated for today.'[51]

This raises two central questions. First, what are the alleged 'coherent foundations' that supposedly underlie the byzantine restrictions and exemptions of the Shops Act 1950? Second, how can these principles be applied to produce a 'polished and updated' set of regulations for today?

The REST Principles

The KSSC claims that the coherent foundations of the present law applying to England and Wales are their own proclaimed REST principles – the idea that retailed goods should in general *not* legally be available to the public on Sundays in England and Wales (although the same goods could be legally sold in Scotland) *unless* they fall into one of the categories allowed under the acronym 'REST', standing for Recreation, Emergencies, Social Gatherings and Travel Requirements.

It is claimed that the curious pattern of exemptions relating to Sunday trading embedded in the Shops Act makes sense under the REST categories in terms of the style of life of a

---

50 *Editor's note.* As this *Hobart Paper* was going to press, it was reported that supporters of the KSSC and the RSAR models had 'joined forces' – see 'The Last-Minute Merger of KSSC and RSAR Models' at the end of this Section, p.51.

51 KSSC, *The REST Principles: How to Update the Law on Sunday Trading,* Cambridge: Jubilee Centre Publications, 1987, p.13.

bygone age. This seems far-fetched;[52] but the KSSC cedes the argument that (whatever its origins) Part IV of the Shops Act 1950 is long out of date and that new legislation is required to bring these regulations into line with contemporary realities on the REST principles.

Behind the REST principles lie three more fundamental goals:

○ To keep Sunday as a special day distinct in character from other days;

○ To promote family life and community gatherings via the vehicle of Sunday 'specialness'; and

○ To protect shopworkers and small shopkeepers from pressure to work on Sundays, and residents near shopping centres from the disamenity of Sunday trading.

These primary goals could not be obtained entirely by restricting exempted goods to those allowable under the REST categories: *the KSSC wants the majority of shops to be closed on Sundays.* The KSSC model, indeed, revolves around the presumption that shops (in England and Wales) *would* be shut *unless* allowed to open on REST criteria.

Operationalising the REST Principles: Some Problems

A general problem with this approach is that of operationalising the broad REST categories in a way that leads to the 'special' Sunday. Take, for example, the criterion of the 'recreational' exemption to a general Sunday trading prohibition. It cannot be denied that the atmosphere at, for example, Camden Lock in London, based on the large market there, is on Sundays very festive. It also constitutes a sort of community gathering. No doubt many young people go there on Sunday for recreational as well as purchasing

---

52 The KSSC has been unable to cite any evidence that the framers of the Shops Act 1950 had these categories in mind when composing Schedule V. As explained in Section II, the Act was but a 'temporary' consolidating measure with no other end in view.

purposes. Yet it is also one of the manifestations of Sunday recreation that the KSSC wants to see driven out of existence.[53]

More generally, as the KSSC itself admits:

> '...the range of goods connected in some way with leisure is so wide as to include nearly all goods – or can easily be interpreted to do so.'[54]

To the deregulationist this is a non-problem. To KSSC supporters it is a fundamental problem as their object is to keep the number of shops opening on a Sunday to a minimum in order to maintain or achieve its desired special character.

The Mark 1 KSSC Model: The Powell Bill

A first attempt at this tricky problem was made in Mr Ray Powell's Shops (Amendment) Bill of 1992.[55] This proposed a complicated system of four classes (A through D) of 'registerable' shops (plus a category of exempt shops) that could be allowed to open on Sundays in England and Wales. As many shops, however, are mixed shops in terms of the product lines purveyed, the Powell Bill also stipulated a so-called '80/20 rule', that is, the turnover attributable to registerable categories would have to constitute a minimum of 80 per cent of the total annual turnover of the shop.

This Private Member's Bill failed in the House of Commons at its Report Stage in May 1993. The local authorities – which will retain the responsibility for administering and enforcing any system of Sunday trading regulation – also reacted strongly against it on grounds of impracticality: '...they considered the Shops (Amendment) Bill and, in particular, the 80/20 turnover rule "virtually unworkable"' (Cm. 2300, para.45).

To overcome these problems (and perhaps also for other reasons noted earlier in this Section), the KSSC option presented in Cm. 2300 is a redesigned model.

---

53 The KSSC model proposes that 'markets comprising more than five stalls will be required to close unless the right to hold a market has been acquired by virtue of a grant or an enactment or order' (Cm. 2300, para.36).

54 KSSC, *The REST Principles, op. cit.*, p.7.

55 Mr Powell is a KSSC supporter and USDAW-sponsored MP.

The KSSC model was altered in yet further ways over the Summer of 1993, after the publication of Cm.2300. These additional changes, however, are not substantive, and were not in published form at the time of writing. The exposition of 'the' KSSC model below is therefore based on that elaborated in Cm. 2300, this being the most recent published version available. The further modifications are described and discussed at the end of this Section (below, pp.49-51).

The Reformulated KSSC Model, Draft Bill Vintage

The redesigned KSSC model in Cm. 2300, like the Mark 1 prototype, is based upon the general presumption that any shop in England and Wales will be closed, by law, on Sundays *unless* it meets certain criteria for *exemption*, or falls into the category of larger *registered* shops that are permitted to trade on narrowly-defined registration criteria.

The proposed allowable types of exempt shops are those which are exempt, irrespective of size (shown in Box B), and those which fall into the allowable category of size-limited exempt shops (listed in Box C). The criteria for the latter are that they must be less than 280 square metres in floor size, and that their principal activity must fall within the designated generic classes laid out in Box C. Additionally, the KSSC model envisages some small shops being allowed to open in England and Wales by virtue of their highly specific location, if in accordance with the categories stipulated in Box D.

Registerable Larger Shops

In addition to the foregoing categories of small shops that may trade at any time on Sundays in England and Wales (provided their principal activity falls within the defined bounds), under the KSSC model in Cm.2300 format some restricted categories of shops larger than the 280 square metres threshold may be allowed to open (between 9 a.m. and 8 p.m.), subject to certain rigorous conditions. These are that:

O The shop must be eligible for registration with the local authority.

O Eligibility for registration is confined to three classes of large shops only – garden centres (class A), motor/cycle supplies shops (class B), and DIY shops (class C).

[39]

KSSC Model

Shops which are exempt irrespective of size:

- **Off-licences, Pubs, Restaurants** and **Take-Aways**

- **Chemists** selling medicines

- **Petrol Filling Stations**

But the shop must not exceed 280 sq. metres excluding the petrol pump area.

- **Vehicle Hire Shops**

- **Shops at Airports**

- **Bureaux de Change** and **Banks**

But only for the sale of foreign currency and trans-actions involving travellers' cheques.

- **Post Offices**

But only for postal services.

- **Funeral Undertakers**

Source: Cm.2300

o To be eligible for registration the principal activity of the shops must also be as defined by the relevant categories for these types of shops shown in Box C.

o The items which these shops are permitted to sell are *also* restricted to the items allowed under their principal activity (so, for example, a DIY shop could probably not sell a roll of carpet, and definitely not a lampshade on a Sunday; but it could retail bricks and wallpaper).

Box C

KSSC Model

Size-Limited Exempt Shops (280 sq.m. max):

- **General Convenience Stores**

Principal Activity is the sale of Groceries, domestic cleaning materials and confectionery.

- **Newsagent**

Principal Activity is the sale of newspapers and confectionery.

- **Video Hire Shops**

Principal Activity is the sale or hire of video recordings.

- **'Mixed' Shops**

Mixture must be of the three above.

- **Florists**

Principal Activity is the sale of cut flowers.

- **Garden Centres**

Principal Activity is the sale of plants, garden supplies and accessories.

- **Motor Supplies Shops**

Principal Activity is the sale of motor or cycle supplies and accessories.

- **DIY Shops**

Principal Activity is the sale of material and tools for the construction, decoration or repair of dwellings.

- **Chemist's Shops**

Principal Activity is the sale of medicinal products, surgical appliances, toiletries and cosmetics.

- **Farm Shops**

Principal Activity is the sale of home-grown produce.

- **Kiosks** and **Stalls**

No more than 10 sq.m, except as part of a market.

Source: Cm.2300

KSSC Model

Small Shops exempted by virtue of location:

- Certain **Tourist Shops**

But the Principal Activity must be the sale of souvenirs and 'goods having some local association'.

- **Shops at hospitals**

- **Shops in Sports Centres** or **places where games are conducted**

But the Principal Activity must be the sale or hire of goods directly connected with the sport or game carried on there.

- **Railway Station Shops**

But the Principal Activity must be the sale of books, newspapers or periodicals.

- **Kiosks in Theatres/Cinemas**

But Principal Activity must be either/or both the sale of programmes and confectionery.

Source: Cm.2300

Outside the foregoing restrictions, shops would not be legally able to open for business on Sundays in England and Wales under the KSSC model, and would face fines of up to £50,000 for breaching this new criminal law (some 20 times larger than the maximum fine under the current Shops Act for trading on Sundays outside the terms of that Act). It is the clear and deliberate intention of this model, in other words, to keep the doors of a large variety of shops very firmly closed on Sundays in England and Wales. Those categories of shops which would not be allowed to open at all under the KSSC model – as specified in Cm. 2300 – are listed in Box E.

KSSC Model

Shops which must close on Sundays in England and Wales, but not in Scotland, include:

- Supermarkets
- Gas Showrooms
- Department Stores
- Craft Shops
- Estate Agents
- Butchers, Bakers, Fruiterers and other specialist shops
- Shoe Shops
- Pet Shops
- Book Shops
- Curtain/Blind Shops
- Toy Shops
- Glassware and China Shops
- Travel Agents
- Auctions
- White Goods Shops
- Stationers
- Furniture Shops
- Confectioners
- Kitchen Shops
- Car Showrooms
- Antique Shops
- Carpet Shops
- Banks
- Clothes Shops
- Record Shops
- Charity Shops
- Sunday Markets (of more than 5 stalls)

Source: Cm.2300

2. The RSAR Model

As explained earlier (p.31), the RSAR was formed (led by M & S) only in late 1992, and its proposals are very much the 'Johnny-come-lately' of the four policy options considered in the Draft Bill. The RSAR model is therefore the least explicitly developed of the four, both in terms of its intellectual foundations and its precise implications for policy; indeed, there is at the time of writing little or no written material on it to which the student may be referred.[56] Cm. 2300 informs us that the model was to be in 'process of development' over the Summer of 1993, and the resulting changes to 'the' RSAR model are detailed and discussed at the end of this Section (below, pp.50-51). As with the changes to 'the' KSSC model (also described at the end of this Section), these further mutations of the RSAR proposals are matters of nuance rather than substance. Moreover, the only published blueprint of 'the' RSAR model at the time of writing was that in Cm. 2300. Accordingly, the description of 'the' RSAR elaborated immediately below is based upon the specification in that White Paper.

According to Cm. 2300, 'the [RSAR] model is based upon the KSSC model' and the general intention of the RSAR is to offer 'a regulatory option which is not quite as strict as that provided by the KSSC'. Our description of the RSAR model may accordingly be brief. It adopts from the KSSC model (in their Cm. 2300 formats):

o The same general framework of exemption and registration for the proposed constriction of Sunday trading in England and Wales.

o The same definition of classes A, B and C large shops that would be eligible to trade in England and Wales on Sundays (that is, DIY stores, garden centres and motor supplies shops).

o The same idea of a 'principal activity' to define the nature of a shop (and thus whether it may enter the exemption or registerable categories).

o The same maximum penalty (a £50,000 fine) in respect of a detected transgression.

---

56 The following articulation of the RSAR model draws upon 'Retailers for Shops Act Reform: Key Proposals', London: RSAR, 1993; and 'Retailers for Shops Act Reform: The Compromise Solution to Sunday Trading', London: RSAR, 1993.

o The same dichotomy of regulatory intent as between England/Wales on the one hand and Scotland on the other – the model is proposed for the former, but not for the latter (where the continuation of full deregulation is the implicit assumption of the model).

There are, however, a number of differentiating features as between the RSAR and KSSC models as presented in Cm. 2300, detailed in Box F.[57]

3. Some Problems with the KSSC and RSAR Models

Given the considerable overlap between both the content and the approach of the KSSC and RSAR models, they raise similar problems. For example:

The Enduring Problem of Anomalies

One of the intentions of these models is to update the schema of Sunday trading restriction by the removal of anomalies that emerged under the Shops Act 1950. Any system of discriminatory regulation will, however, create anomalies. The KSSC and RSAR models do not overcome these problems: they simply promise to swap new anomalies for old ones. As Cm. 2300 (p.11) notes in respect of the KSSC model:

> 'It would mean [if implemented] that a DIY store of 270 square metres could sell its full product range, but one of 290 square metres could risk prosecution for selling products identical to those sold by its small competitor.'

The RSAR variant would avoid this particular anomaly because of the absence in their model (see Box F) of the proposed KSSC restrictions on the items that registered stores may purvey on Sundays. But it creates *other* anomalies. For example, under its proposals garden centres will be able to sell china and glassware on Sunday, whereas china and glass shops will not. Craft shops will be able to sell shoes and toys, but shoe shops and toy shops will be prevented from opening. A convenience store in the suburbs will be able to sell tights and socks on Sundays; Sock Shops at railway stations will not

---

57 A further one is that the RSAR proposes that trading which breaches the conditions of registration would be dealt with by revocation of registration; only if a shop continued to trade in breach would an offence be committed.

Box F

RSAR Model

Differences from the KSSC Model:

- **Wine Warehouses** may open

Add to Box B.

- **Antique/Craft Shops** may open

Add to Box C, delete from Box E.

- **Sunday Markets** permitted

Add to Box B, delete from Box E.

- **Banks, Travel Agents** and **Estate Agents** may open

Add to Box B, delete from Box E.

- **Registered A/B/C Larger Stores**

Sunday sales not restricted to authorised items as stipulated in the KSSC model.

- **Four Open Sundays before Christmas**

All shops may open.

Source: Cm.2300

(although the latter would be possible under the RSAR model if it were instead located at a seaport or airport).

A More Glaring Anomaly?

Both models would retain the different regulatory framework for Sunday trading as between Scotland on the one hand, and England and Wales on the other. Indeed, the differences would increase. It seems odd to intensify the disparity of economic laws between the regions of a unitary state and a unified economic area. Over recent years the differences

[46]

between England and Wales and Scotland have been eroded because Part IV of the Shops Act 1950 has fallen increasingly into 'desuetude' (to use the Scottish legal term). But advocates of these models propose to resurrect and reinforce the differences, by the establishment of a new registration system south of the Border, backed by penal fines.

This raises questions of anomalies far more profound than the distortions of cross-border retailing competition that are likely to ensue.[58] Most people would regard as anomalous different banking laws on opposite sides of the Pennines. Why then have different Sunday trading laws in Gwynedd and Glasgow?[59] If the arguments for applying a tough regulatory framework on Sunday trading – making breach a severe criminal offence – hold good for Cumbria, why not for Dumfries?

The answer of the KSSC, at least, seems to be that there are differences in underlying socio-economic characteristics:

> 'England has a far higher population density, and a larger proportion of households with cars than Scotland, making Sunday trading more attractive.'[60]

The implication appears to be that the English and Welsh need to be restrained by regulation from voluntary retail exchange on Sundays in ways that the Scots do not – *if* we are to presume, as the KSSC does, that Sunday trading constitutes a public 'bad' in the technical economic sense.

However, even if we consider voluntary retail exchange on Sundays to be a bad thing, it would not be correct to apply different laws north and south of the Border. The severity of pollution, as with Sunday trading, is also related positively to car and population densities. Yet we have precisely the same

---

58 Sunday trading restrictions in the Canadian provinces of Ontario and British Columbia cause a significant diversion of Sunday retail trade to neighbouring American states.

59 The same argument could of course apply to the local authority autonomy model discussed earlier. As also noted earlier, however, there is both theoretical reason and empirical evidence to support the view that the process of regulatory competition between small and adjacent local authorities would bring about a considerable degree of homogeneity in regulation; a dichotomy imposed by a national statute cannot be tempered by competitive forces in the same way.

60 S. Burton-Jones, *New Facts for Auld*, Cambridge: Jubilee Centre Publications, 1989, p.57.

general framework of environmental law and controls on both sides of the Scottish border – because pollution is pollution wherever it occurs. At the very minimum, a reasonably consistent application of the KSSC/RSAR line of economic argument would be that the tough regulatory policies that they now advocate for Birmingham, Manchester and London need to be applied with equal vigour to those carbound, urban areas of Scotland that show similar proclivities to indulge in Sunday shopping, for, as KSSC research has revealed:

> '53 per cent of shops in Edinburgh and Glasgow that opened on Sunday [in 1987] were open on every Sunday. This compares with less than 20 per cent in the rest of Scotland.'[61]

Conversely, if there is a case for allowing deregulation in rural Scotland on the grounds that Sunday trading is unlikely to be at 'damaging' levels there, why does not the same case also apply to the counties of Gwynedd, Dyfed, Northumberland and Norfolk?

The Determination of a Shop's 'Principal Activity'

The original KSSC (Powell Bill) formulation of the test of a store's business relied on the '80/20 rule'. This rule was much criticised in parliamentary discussion of the Bill, and was also rejected generally by local authorities as unenforceable. To circumvent such criticism the Cm. 2300 variants of the KSSC and RSAR models, as described above, dispense with any rigid 80/20 rule and talk instead of a shop's 'principal' activity. The Draft Bill, however, contains no definition of this term. What does it mean in business and economic reality?

The concept (according to the KSSC) has been created to give a degree of flexibility in these matters that a strict accounting rule of the 80/20 (or 75/25, for instance) variety cannot provide. It is not supposed to relate (entirely) to the shop's annual turnover; and the general idea is that a variety of factors would have to be taken into account (by local authorities and, ultimately, the courts), such as the shop's stock situation, its purchase orders, areas of display, and the 'general feeling of the shop'.[62] This formulation is

---

61 S. Burton-Jones, *op.cit.*, p.55.

62 E.g., does this 'feel' like a DIY shop, or a convenience store?

undoubtedly very flexible – to the point of being stretchable into endless contortions. It is possible to see much litigation arising, with shoppers and shopkeepers, local authority officers and – not least – the courts themselves having difficulty in appreciating the subtleties of different magistrates' and judicial rulings on such subjective matters.

Proponents of the KSSC/RSAR schemes hazard the guess that the courts might eventually come to some rough rule of thumb to overcome these problems in defining a shop's principal activity – perhaps, 51 per cent of its annual turnover. This, however, must remain a guess. As things stand, if the KSSC or RSAR regulatory schemes are to be passed by Parliament with such a vague, 'flexible' definition of a shop's principal activity, the resulting long-awaited 'reform' of Sunday trading in England and Wales would not simply sweep away the anomalies and pettifogging anachronisms associated with the Shops Act 1950. It would open up a Pandora's Box of questions relating to the legality of Sunday trading in England and Wales, because of the slippery and contentious nature of the principal activity concept.

4. Some Interim Conclusions

There are further criticisms of these regulatory models for Sunday trading which are addressed in Section V as components of the positive case for a deregulatory approach. Even on their own grounds, however, it is clear that it is difficult to 'update and polish' the Shops Act 1950 without intensifying, and indeed creating, many anomalies.

*   *   *

Late Changes to 'the' KSSC and RSAR Models

As noted above, the KSSC and RSAR models were in a state of flux, both before and after the publication of Cm.2300 in July 1993. This tailpiece notes and comments upon the further changes in their specifications that were made over the Summer of 1993. The late appearance of these alterations underlines the fluidity of these matters.

KSSC Model: Further Changes

In the 'final' KSSC model:

(i) The requirement that larger shops opening on Sundays in England and Wales must register with their local authority is dropped.

(ii) The definition of a 'shop' is restricted so that banks, building societies and estate agents would be able to open without restraint on Sundays.

(iii) The 'principal activity' test for defining a shop's business is replaced by that of what their business is 'wholly or mainly'.

These are not substantial changes. With regard to (i), it is to be noted that all of the other restrictive conditions applying to large shops opening under a KSSC régime would remain. For example, only those large shops which principally retailed either DIY, garden or motor/cycle supplies would be eligible to open on Sundays, and then only to sell permitted items (not their full product range). Turning to (ii), the deletions noted – as can be seen from Box E – do not alter the fact that many types of shop would still be prevented from opening under the new KSSC régime. Finally, as regards (iii) the change in phraseology does not solve the central problem that local authorities, retailers, and ultimately the courts would face a difficult (and expensive) task in applying these vague terms to the complex realities of modern retail operations. This matter is elaborated further in sub-section (v) of the next Section of this *Hobart Paper*.

RSAR Model: Further Changes

In the 'final' RSAR model:

(a) The requirement of registration for larger shops to open on Sundays in England and Wales is likewise dropped, although the other restrictions on large shop opening stipulated in the RSAR model (Cm. 2300 version) would continue to apply.

(b) Shops that are exempted from the restriction of Sunday opening are to be defined by their generic labels (e.g., 'convenience store', 'wine warehouse', 'antique/craft shop') with no attempt further to define these categories in terms of their 'whole', 'main', or 'principal' activity. It would be left to the courts to decide on these problems via actual cases brought before them.

The same general comments made concerning alterations (i) and (iii) in the KSSC model also apply to changes (a) and (b) in the RSAR model.

The Last-Minute Merger of the KSSC and RSAR Models

As this *Hobart Paper* was going to press, it was announced in the Queen's Speech of 18 November 1993 that the Sunday Trading Bill 1993 presenting the options for reform for Parliamentary decision offers a menu of only three alternatives (and not four, as set out in Cm.2300). This results from a last minute, behind-the-scenes merger of the KSSC and RSAR models.

As with all political horse-trades, both elements have had to compromise on some of their tenets. In the 'merged model', the KSSC has conceded to the RSAR that all shops should be allowed to open for the four Sundays before Christmas, and that Sunday markets and 'car boot' sales would be allowed. Conversely, the RSAR has ceded to the KSSC the principle that the restricted categories (A, B, C, as above) of larger shops permitted to open on Sundays in England and Wales would be further restricted by law to purveying only certain specified types of product (as laid down in 'the' KSSC above). The merged model also rests upon the idea, originated by the KSSC over the Summer of 1993, that the test for defining a shop's business for the purposes of this model rests on the concept of what the business is 'wholly or mainly'.

The purpose of this merger is, of course, to obtain political synergy from combination. None of the changes, however, deflect the basic criticisms regarding regulatory approaches to reform made above. Furthermore, the merged KSSC/RSAR model is open to the charge that some of its main features are, apparently, the result of vote-maximising considerations rather than either principle or considerations of regulatory effectiveness and efficiency.

V. DEREGULATORY APPROACHES TO REFORM

The Government's *Guide to the Options for Reform* sets out two deregulatory approaches: full deregulation of Sunday trading to bring the legal situation in England and Wales into line with that in Scotland; and partial deregulation in the specific form proposed by the Shopping Hours Reform Council (SHRC).

This Section elaborates these options and their likely effects, and the arguments for deregulation.

1. The Deregulation Model

Deregulation has the considerable attraction of overriding the costs and difficulties of administration and law enforcement associated with regulatory schemes. Shoppers and shop managers would simply decide whether or not to engage in trading on Sundays.

There is some uncertainty about the future pattern of opening that would result from deregulation in England and Wales, although the indications from current patterns of opening are that this would generally be above current Scottish levels (where as a rough rule of thumb, approximately 25 per cent of shops open on Sundays, with more on the Sundays preceding Christmas). Indeed, a MORI Poll conducted in England and Wales in 1992 suggested that 29 per cent of shops were already open on Sundays, though a London Economics estimate (based on a survey of some 200 shops/multiples representing 11,000 outlets conducted at end-1992/early 1993) suggested a much higher average of 38 per cent, rising to 46 per cent in the case of food sector retail outlets (and 85 per cent for the drink, confectionery and tobacco sector).

This level of Sunday trading could, of course, be an over-estimate due to biased sampling; equally, it could be an under-estimate of the situation that might emerge over time, as consumers adjust their shopping habits and patterns slowly to the post-deregulation scene.

It is also possible to provide some tentative estimates of the pattern of Sunday opening across retail sectors post-

[52]

deregulation. In 1984, a study undertaken by MORI for the Institute for Fiscal Studies' *Economic Review* as part of the Auld Inquiry found that the most popular products that consumers would like to buy occasionally on Sundays in Great Britain were DIY/decorating materials (40 per cent of respondents), garden products (38 per cent), books and cards (21 per cent), toiletries and cosmetics (17 per cent), and carpets/furniture (13 per cent).

By 1993, however, consumers in England and Wales had much more extensive experience of Sunday opening than they did in 1984, and the potential pattern of demand post-deregulation may not be entirely the same now as it seemed almost a decade ago. Box G, which reproduces the findings of a survey of 1,710 adults sampled for their intentions at 142 points in England and Wales in November 1992 by MORI/London Economics,[63] gives some indication of the possible shape of Sunday retail demand post-deregulation.

The figures in Box G should be taken as indicative only. The future is essentially unknowable; and there are well-known problems in drawing inferences about actual behaviour from the results of interview studies (however carefully worded). Nevertheless, some tentative conclusions can be drawn.

Still Untapped Potential for Sunday Shopping?

The broad result of this attitude study is that there *could* be still considerable potential growth in demand for Sunday shopping to emerge, once consumers have fully adjusted to the new opportunities. On average, across the five retail sectors identified, this amounts to a more than 100 per cent growth in the proportion of shopping done on Sundays; but this varies widely as between the sectors. For DIY/Garden Centres, there may be little *additional* demand as a result of a fully-deregulated Sunday because – whether legally, illegally, or in a grey legal area – this sector has been increasingly open on Sundays from the latter half of the 1980s onwards in Great Britain. Both the household/electrical and grocery sectors, however, show the potential for a more than doubling of

---

63 As reported in London Economics, *The Economic Impact of Alternative Sunday Trading Régimes: A Report for the Home Office Research and Planning Unit*, London: London Economics, 1993 (mimeo), pp.15-16 (subsequently referred to as 'London Economics Study 1993').

Potential Demand for Sunday Shopping

Question: What proportion of your shopping *would you do* if all shops were open on Sundays?

Type of Shopping	Total (%)	Male (%)	Female (%)	Full-Time Working (%)	Part-Time Working (%)	Not Working (%)	% Increase over actual
Groceries	13·00	13·80	12·70	17·55	14·60	8·85	124
Drink, Confectionery and Tobacco	10·95	12·05	9·60	13·70	10·15	8·10	67
Clothing and Footwear	8·35	9·15	7·45	11·70	9·40	5·65	422
Household/Electrical	10·40	11·95	8·85	15·75	10·60	6·80	129
DIY/Gardening	16·05	18·10	14·90	23·40	18·60	9·85	18
Average, Five Sectors	11·84	12·89	11·05	16·29	12·86	8·03	110

Source: London Economics, 1993, Table 2.5.2

demand for Sunday shopping compared with the current position; and in the clothing and footwear sector there is the prospect of a quadrupling of such demand.

Proponents of regulatory schemes for the reform of Sunday trading would, of course, see such projections as reinforcing their case for a strict clampdown on Sunday trading. Deregulators would argue to the contrary that these results underline the size of the infringement of personal liberty (witnessed in pent-up, potential demand) involved in any enforcement of Sunday trading restrictions.

New Patterns of Sunday Shopping Emerging?

According to London Economics' estimates, shoppers in England and Wales in late 1992 were undertaking 5·8 per cent of their food shopping on Sundays, but only 1·6 per cent of their shopping for clothing and footwear on that day. As far back as 1984, however, when supermarkets, shoe shops and clothing shops were generally shut on Sundays in England and Wales, the Institute for Fiscal Studies (IFS) estimated that there existed a considerable demand for such a shopping opportunity: 'We calculate that if all shops were open on Sundays consumers' present intentions would be to buy 9 per cent of their food and 16 per cent of their clothing on that day'.[64] And the results detailed in Box G indicate that there is a strong additional current demand for food purchasing on Sundays in particular, suggesting a doubling of the current level in percentage terms.

The regulatory options examined in the previous Section would not permit the desired pattern of Sunday shopping to emerge – as would deregulation – and indeed would imply a strong cutback in the level of supermarket shopping on Sundays that currently prevails in England and Wales.

Differing Valuations of Sunday Shopping

Box G also reveals that the demand for Sunday shopping is concentrated strongly on those who are working, rather than

---

64 *The Regulation of Retail Trading Hours: Economic Review Conducted for the Home Office into Proposals to Amend the Shops Acts*, London: IFS, 1984, para. 81. The IFS also found that for food and clothing the potential demand for Sunday shopping was 'significantly greater' in London and the South-East than in other regions of Great Britain.

those who are not – such as the elderly and the unemployed (for whom weekday shop opening hours may be adequate).[65]

2. The SHRC Model: Partial Deregulation

Having considered the implications for the pattern and extent of shop opening on Sundays in England and Wales of full adjustment to deregulation in line with Scotland, we turn to the SHRC model which represents partial deregulation, based on the premise of the SHRC that it is

> 'possible to provide reasonable opportunities for shopping on Sundays while retaining Sunday as a day which is different from the remainder of the week'.[66]

The main elements in the SHRC approach are set out in Box H. Like the KSSC and RSAR models, it creates a dividing line between shops smaller and larger than a floorspace of 280 square metres, with the former being allowed to open at any and all times on Sundays, and the latter subject to some restrictions as stipulated in Box G (unless in the specified exempted class of larger shops that consists of shops at railway stations and airports; registered pharmacies, pubs, restaurants and filling stations).

Regulations relating to larger shops would under the SHRC model be enforced by penalties for offences ranging up to £5,000.

The Effects of Partial Deregulation

Supporters of the RSAR and KSSC schemes claim that the SHRC model is a 'thinly disguised version of *total* deregulation'.[67] But the 6-hour time constraint (see Box H) could critically affect the calculation as to whether a large shop (depending, for example, on its product range and location) would find it profitable to open on a Sunday under SHRC conditions.

---

65 The IFS 1984 study (*op.cit.*) revealed the same result (Table 3.8). Such differences are entirely consistent with the economic analysis of the allocation of time, and which forms a component of the substantive case for deregulation in economic terms (as developed later – see below, pp.64-67).

66 Cm. 2300, para. 11.

67 Retailers for Shops Act Reform, 'The Compromise Solution to Sunday Trading', London: RSAR, 1993 (mimeo, p.1).

SHRC Model

Small Shops (under 280 sq.m.):

- Free to open at all times on Sundays

Larger Shops (over 280 sq.m.):

- May only open legally on Sundays between 10am and 6pm and if they:
  - ➢ Open for a continuous, 6-hour period that is displayed.
  - ➢ Notify the local authority, 14 days in advance, of the selected 6-hour slot.

Exempted larger shops (not constrained to 6 hours or 10am-6pm) include:

- Pubs
- Filling Stations
- Restaurants

All Types of Shops:

- May sell their full range without restriction.

Source: Cm.2300

According to simulation estimates in the London Economics study, implementation of the SHRC proposals would not lead to the same pattern and extent of shop opening times on Sundays in England and Wales as would full deregulation. It would, however, go some way towards stimulating extra opening as compared to the position today, whereas implementation of the KSSC and RSAR options would lead to a substantial degree of Sunday shop closure in comparison with today. These estimates – which should be

TABLE 1
ESTIMATED PROPORTION OF RETAIL
CAPACITY OPEN ON SUNDAYS*
(*per cent*)

Under	Food	Non-Food
Today's Régime	46.0	34.0
Deregulation	75.7	56.3
SHRC	59.3	40.5
RSAR	17.6	16.1
KSSC	5.7	5.0

Source: London Economics, 1993
* Estimates for England and Wales only.

viewed with much caution (like all estimates generated by simulation from a crude econometric model of a complex reality) – are set out in Table 1.[68] They are compared with today's régime – the curious mixture of regulations embedded in the Shops Act 1950 and the effective, partial deregulation that currently obtains in England and Wales.

The SHRC model is something of a halfway house to full deregulation in other respects, too. First, whilst it would not lead to such anomalies as in the KSSC and RSAR models, it does not entirely avoid such problems. It would still, for example, be the case that an electrical shop of 290 square metres would be confined to a 6-hour opening period on a Sunday whilst one of 270 square metres would not be so constrained.

The 280 square metre rule (common to the SHRC, RSAR and KSSC models) is in any case arbitrary because it is *floorspace close to shop frontage* which is most valuable in terms of

---

68 The London Economics Study was undertaken at the stage during which the Powell Bill was in progress in Parliament, and well before Cm. 2300 appeared. It did not in fact examine (as Table 1 would suggest) *the* KSSC option, but rather *two* Powell Bill variants – a 'tight' and a 'liberal' interpretation of the Bill's intentions. For the sake of comparison, Table 1 utilises the London Economics estimates of the Powell Bill (liberal) impacts as a guide to what might transpire if the KSSC option elaborated in Cm. 2300 were to be introduced.

revenue-generation; a shop which is deep but has only a narrow frontage of 280 square metres has nowhere near the same trading potential as one with the same floorspace but a long frontage and a shallow interior. This market reality underlies the 'zoning principle', mainly adopted in retail rent determinations in the UK.[69] All three models arbitrarily assume that the gross internal square footage of a shop is an accurate guide to its (Sunday) trading potential, which is clearly not true.

Furthermore, implementation of the SHRC model would not obviate the anomalies arising from different Sunday trading legislation applying to shops on opposite sides of the Scottish border. The SHRC model would much reduce this glaring anomaly, whereas the KSSC and RSAR models would intensify it considerably; nevertheless, a perceptible anomaly would remain. A store seeking to open south of the Border on Sundays would be subject to regulations about notifying the local authority (on pain of a not inconsiderable fine).

These specific points underline a general question about the logic of the SHRC model: if the intention is to move in the direction of deregulation, why not go the whole way and provide a unified framework of full deregulation of Sunday trading throughout Great Britain? Conversely, what is the rationalisation for the anomalies and restrictions that remain in this model of partial deregulation?

Compared with the KSSC and RSAR models, the SHRC approach would undoubtedly be relatively easy for local government to operate and enforce. As with all 'halfway houses', however, the question remains whether it is a half-baked concept, lacking the clearer foundations of more radical reforms.

3. The Arguments for Deregulation

The basic argument for full deregulation of Sunday trading in England and Wales is that it is a popular and libertarian prospect: 'opinion polls show that about two-thirds of the public want to be able to shop on Sundays'.[70] There are, however, some more subtle economic arguments for full

---

69 See J. Burton, *Retail Rents: Fair and Free Market?*, London: Adam Smith Institute, 1992, Appendix: 'Behind the Comparables'.

70 Cm. 2300, para. 4.

deregulation in this arena of commercial activity which are, perhaps, not so readily apparent. These are elaborated in the five sub-sections that follow.

(i) Equality of Regulatory Treatment

There is a fundamental case to be made for the equal treatment of enterprises and industries in respect of regulation and other forms of government intervention. Deviations from this general principle need to be justified on clear-cut grounds.

It is not obvious why it should be that the retail trade is the one form of commerce singled out in English and Welsh regulation (but not in Scotland) for exceptional constraint on Sundays. As matters stand, retailing (of certain goods) is one of the *very* few activities which is prohibited on a Sunday in England and Wales. In their capacities as consumers, people in England and Wales are, on that day, free to shop in principle – it is the serving of such customers (except for exempt items) which is made illegal by the Shops Act. More generally, there are no laws restraining other types of trade or commerce. It is quite legal for offices to open all day long on Sundays, and for manufacturing plants to work flat out. It is quite legal for entertainments businesses such as cinemas and stately homes – and indeed strip clubs – to operate. In their capacity as employees or entrepreneurs, the English and Welsh are completely free to work on Sunday in any service or manufacturing endeavour that they wish other than those parts of the retail trade which are affected by the present restrictions.[71]

Even more specifically, the rest of the distribution system, including the wholesale trade, and delivery services to retail outlets, operates without restraint under the Shops Act 1950 – and would continue to do so under both the KSSC and RSAR models. Major food retailers – including Marks & Spencer, the prime campaigner in the RSAR lobby – take deliveries of foods (in particular chilled and frozen) on a 24-hours-a-day, seven-days-a-week basis.

If the intention is to 'keep Sunday special', it is not clear why the REST criteria apparently apply only to retailing, and not to manufacturing, office work and wholesaling. *Prima*

---

71 Cm. 2300 estimates (para. 7) that there are some 5 million Britons currently working on Sundays; some other estimates run much higher.

facie, this discrimination against a particular industry has no economic justification.

(ii) Regulatory Discrimination in Evolutionary Perspective

This problem of regulatory discrimination becomes all the more obvious once we recognise the essentially evolutionary character of the market process.[72] It is part and parcel of this process that because of the drive for innovation, new products (previously unperceived by the framers of the regulatory schema) are emerging all of the time. Retailing (standing between ultimate consumers and manufacturers in the supply chain) is at the cutting edge of this ceaseless and significant process of new product innovation. As one historian of shopping noted almost two decades ago:

> 'It is astonishing to realise that over half the goods being sold in modern shops are postwar discoveries. How did people manage to live without detergents, frozen foods, plastic kitchenware, paper handkerchiefs, non-iron shirts, creaseless skirts, fake furs, laminated surfaces, spin driers, nylon tights, ball-point pens, instant coffee, transistor radio sets, electric showers, and much else besides?'[73]

It would, of course, be necessary today to add greatly to this list – for example, the cornucopia of new products that has emerged in the field of consumer electronics.

At the same time as new products emerge, others wither away and disappear because of changes in demand, in taste, technology and cost. For instance, the demand for 'partly cooked tripe' – exempted under the Fifth Schedule of the Shops Act – is not as it once was (it is probably now not sold anywhere at all in England and Wales on Sundays).

As a result of this continuous process of evolutionary change in the array of products on offer in a market economy, any regulations with exemptions based on specified

---

72 Relevant perspectives on the evolutionary character of the market economy are variously contained in R.R. Nelson and S.G. Winter, *An Evolutionary Theory of Economic Change,* Cambridge, Mass: Harvard University Press, 1982; M.L. Rothschild, *Bionomics: The Inevitability of Capitalism,* London: Futura, 1992; and in a substantial selection of writings by members of the school of (neo-) Austrian economics, e.g. I.M. Kirzner, *Discovery and the Capitalist Process,* Chicago: University of Chicago Press, 1985.

73 M. Harrison, *People and Shopping: A Social Background,* London: Ernest Benn, 1975, p.138.

goods stipulated at a point in time (as with the Shops Act 1950) must fall into *ever-increasing* disrepair and disrepute with the passage of time, as previously non-existent anomalies are continuously added to the original distortions created by the scheme.

(iii) The Chimera of Alternative Exemption Criteria

Perhaps in recognition of this fundamental problem, the efforts to 'polish and update' the Shops Act embodied in the KSSC and RSAR models represent an attempt to move away from a principle of exemption based upon statutorily stipulated goods to one founded upon *exemption by type of shop*.

Does this not avoid the problem of increasingly arbitrary discrimination because of the emergence of new goods over time? We have already noted in Section IV that the attempt to avoid specifying goods has led to the move in these models to define types of shop not in terms of concrete products but rather via vague and open-ended concepts such as the 'principal activity' of a shop or what its business 'wholly or mainly' is. This is likely to give rise to considerable and costly litigation (see sub-section (v) below). Moreover, the KSSC model in particular represents only a *partial* escape from a principle of exemption based upon specified goods. This is so because to qualify for exemption in these proposals, a large shop (of more than 280 square metres) must not only be of a specific type and with a permitted category of products, but also will then only be allowed to sell *certain* of these goods on Sunday. The RSAR model avoids the latter difficulty by *not* restricting large exempt shops to the sale of authorised goods on Sunday; nevertheless, there is a more fundamental problem embedded in both varieties of regulatory proposal.

Competition in Retail Formats

The competitive process is not simply one involving goods; it also involves the formats, styles, product ranges, presentational methods, and organisational routines utilised to deliver these goods to consumers. Shoppers therefore make choices, not simply between goods but rather between a *combination* of retail goods and retail formats. The latter include convenience stores, supermarkets, hypermarkets, discounters, department stores, mail-order businesses, large-area specialists, mini-markets, small specialist shops, boutiques, showrooms, kiosks and market stalls. Each embodies a differing competitive strategy, and associated functional strategies (varying in terms of such dimensions as opening times, staff inputs, capital requirements, design and layout inputs, deployment of information technology, advertising and marketing expenditures, location strategy).

The proposed KSSC/RSAR exemption criterion based upon designated types of retail format inevitably discriminates arbitrarily between these formats and their underlying competitive and functional strategies, according (for example) to whether the format concerned falls on one side or another of the proposed 280 square metre dividing line. As with the problems arising from exemptions for specified goods, prospective competitive anomalies need to be seen in an evolutionary rather than a static perspective.

One of the underlying concerns that motivates the regulatory models of the KSSC/RSAR reform proposals is the 'survival of the small shop'. It is one of the truisms of post-war British retailing that there has been a

> 'marked rise in [the] share of national retail trade taken by chain stores or multiples; and a sharp fall in shop numbers with the co-op and one-shop independents showing the largest decline'.[74]

These *historical* trends, however, are not necessarily a guide to the future. Currently, in the UK (and France and Germany) the classic format of the multiple – the self-service supermarket and superstore/hypermarket – is in a decline or maturity phase losing market share to other formats, in particular to discount stores and small convenience stores in the inner cities.[75] Apart from Kwik Save, there were no discounters on the British scene in 1990; there are now some 13.

The supermarkets that the KSSC and RSAR models would close on Sundays (except, in the latter case, on the four before Christmas) offer a format involving one-stop shopping, very large product ranges, piped music, other facilities such as car-parking and restaurants, and state-of-the-art scanners at check-outs. With these additional features go premium prices.

---

74 J.A.N. Bamfield, 'The Changing Face of British Retailing', *National Westminster Bank Quarterly Review*, May 1980, p.33. Note that 'multiples' are defined here as retail groups with 10 or more stores.

75 Eurostat, *Retailing in the European Single Market*, Brussels: Commission of the European Communities, 1993, Ch.4.

This differentiation strategy is vulnerable particularly to the competition of so-called 'hard' deep-discounting of the kind that has flourished in Germany. This is based on the opposite strategy of gaining cost and price leadership by all available means, including few staff, goods sold out of open boxes, a very small product range, minimal stock, and the renting of 'small, cheap sites on street corners in order to get as near to customers as possible'.[76] The deep-discounters would (given small enough size) be able to open on Sundays in England and Wales under the KSSC and RSAR models, whereas what might now be called the 'traditional' British supermarket would be barred from doing so.

It is perhaps not surprising that Aldi – a leading German discounter which already has an extensive presence in UK food retailing – is a supporter of the RSAR model, whilst many 'traditional' supermarket chains (e.g., Sainsbury's, Tesco) support the SHRC proposals. All that this illustrates is that *any* regulatory scheme will have effects that give certain businesses artificial competitive advantages, whilst subjecting others to an imposed competitive hobble. One element in the case for full deregulation is that it is the *only* approach that can provide a level playing field and thus allow the resulting structure of retailing to reflect consumer choice and cost factors rather than the interests of particular retailing groups.

(iv) Sunday Trading and the Economics of Time

We owe to the work of the 1992 Nobel Laureate in Economics, Professor Gary Becker, the insight that households, even in an advanced non-agrarian economy, are not simply composed of consumers; the household is also a production unit combining market goods, own time and other inputs to generate *household-produced* commodities. Moreover, it is the constraint of the time-budget – none of us has more than 168 hours per week, however much we earn in market income – which may be the major limitational factor on choice for many households.[77]

The implication is that the full or true price to a household of any commodity is not simply its monetary price. The full price is composed of two elements: a money price entailed in

---

76 'Europe's Discount Dogfight', *Economist*, 8 May 1993, p.81.

77 The seminal treatment of the general topic is in G.S. Becker, 'A Theory of the Allocation of Time', *Economic Journal*, Vol.75, No.3, September 1965, p.493.

acquiring the goods composed in the household production process, and the 'time price' involved in obtaining and utilising them. In the retail context the time price includes, for example, the time spent in going to shops, comparing items, checking on product quality, and making decisions (such as which carpet shall we buy? Will this one or that one fit best with the decor and furniture?).

Sunday trading restrictions, in whatever model, tend to raise the full price of purchase, by reducing the time opportunities otherwise available and by forcing consumers to substitute other periods of time that may come at a higher opportunity cost in terms of alternatives foregone. Conversely, part of the case for deregulation is that it will *reduce* the full price to households, by allowing them a more extensive and flexible time-budget for shopping and associated activities.

This general argument is particularly significant in the case of those goods which economists describe as 'search goods'. These are products where consumers must indulge in a considerable degree of search activity – that is, inspecting the product (or service) and then comparing it and its specifications with alternatives. These are often of an expensive and complicated nature (as with major DIY items and garden equipment, and electrical appliances such as white goods, photographic equipment and consumer electronics). They may also involve difficult decisions, often of a family nature, relating to the planned usage of the item(s) and the appropriateness of the good in the context of other, often prior, choices (as with carpets, furniture, wallpaper, paint, curtains, bedding). In such cases the time component of the full price of purchase tends to be high, because of the amount of time necessary for comparison and choice – time that may not be readily available (or only at a very high cost) during the week for a full-time employee. Both the KSSC and RSAR models – as can be seen from Boxes E and F – would prevent a considerable volume of search goods from being inspected on Sundays in England and Wales.

The Defence of Shopworkers

Proponents of the REST principles tend to dismiss such time-based arguments for deregulation of Sunday trading on the grounds that it imposes time costs on others, such as shop employees:

[65]

'A person may think of many things he would like to buy on a Sunday. But in many cases he could actually have bought the item earlier in the week. If, despite this, he were allowed to go to the shops and buy the item he wants, someone would have to work on Sunday. The shopworker and the shopworker's family would pay for the *customer's lack of organisation*. Or...it might make little difference if he were to delay the purchase...it can easily wait a day or two. If a shopworker were brought out to work to make the purchase possible, he would be paying for the *customer's impatience*' (italics added).[78]

Taking this argument to its logical conclusion, however, we could by law require that shops open on only one day of the week, allowing shopworkers a very considerable amount of time off, and throwing all of the costs of organising onto customers! Clearly, in a free society the natural outcome would be somewhat different, because the customer would be prepared to pay for the extra service provided by shop employees being around on extra days. All trades involve costs and opportunities foregone to both parties, and Sunday trading is no different in this respect. Trade is possible and mutually beneficial, however, only if the two parties value their alternatives – what they have to forego – differently. It is therefore not surprising to discover (as noted earlier in this Section) that it is those who are in employment (and especially full-time employment) who are particularly keen for Sunday shopping opportunities; the opportunity cost of enforced weekday shopping is highest for this group.

The case for deregulation becomes the more apparent when one takes a long-run, evolutionary perspective on the market system. Over the long run, the workings of this system have raised the average real income of employees greatly (and therefore increased the opportunity cost of not working). But neither the market economy, nor any other form of system, can alter the individual's time-budget constraint from 168 hours per week. Thus economic development over the long run raises the opportunity cost of time remorselessly, generating 'temporal poverty'.[79] This pressure on the

---

78 *The REST Principles*, Cambridge: Keep Sunday Special Campaign, 1987, p.8.

79 S. Burns, *The Household Economy: Its Shape, Origins and Future*, Boston: Beacon Press, 1975, p.173. See also K. Culligan and J. Murphy, 'The Future of Leisure', *Long Range Planning*, Vol.22, No.6, pp.127-31.

household time-budget has been reinforced in the 20th century by the increasing participation of married women in the workforce (where currently 70 per cent of married women work either full- or part-time in the UK). Thus, whilst the opportunity cost of time during the work-week has been rising over the course of economic development, the general availability of time for shopping to the household has simultaneously been falling.

These trends and pressures are simply not going to go away. As we approach the 21st century, it is in the light of these trends that the long-run case for deregulating Sunday trading needs to be especially considered. A panoply of new restrictions on Sunday trading would simply intensify the problems associated with these long-run tendencies in our society and economy. Deregulation cannot, of course, suppress these powerful trends; but it would allow individuals extra flexibility to adapt their behaviour patterns to them.

(v) Sunday Trading Restrictions and the Costs of Regulation

An implicit assumption of the KSSC and RSAR models is that penalties for evasion can and will be set at such draconian levels that evasion of the regulations would be zero or minimal under these new régimes. This same postulate was made explicit in the econometric modelling on the impacts of these proposals in the study undertaken by London Economics, which made the working assumption for simulation purposes that 'contraventions would be rare' if these models were implemented, and thus could be ignored.[80]

The general issue of enforcement *cannot*, however, be safely ignored in deliberating upon the reform options. There is, first, a basic political question to be asked. Even if Parliament were to adopt the KSSC model as the general basis for the reform of the law on Sunday trading, would it necessarily adopt the penal fines that the KSSC advocates as part of the package? The £50,000 fines contemplated (at the upper limit) in the KSSC and RSAR models are immensely larger than magistrates have the power to impose at present, implying that an exceptionally serious crime is involved. The reality, however, is that Sunday trading in England and Wales today is

---

80 London Economics Study, 1993, *op. cit.*, p.26.

a crime *created* by the attempt of governmental authorities to come between willing buyers and willing sellers. Long experience with the Shops Act 1950 should be a warning that the issue of enforcement cannot be swept under the carpet by making unrealistic assumptions about penalty levels and deterrence. The possibility and the cost of enforcement at realistic penalty and policing levels appropriate to the 'crime' involved is a central aspect of the need for reform.

Second, whatever the enforcement régime applied to new regulations, it is not necessarily true that the problem and cost of enforcing them would shrivel to minimal levels. There are hidden complexities involved.

A Stimulus to the Grey Economy?

There has been much discussion over recent years of the 'black economy' which revolves around market transactions that are deliberately hidden from official gaze, either because they are illicit or because concealment permits evasion of taxes and other imposts such as social security 'contributions'. Another, previously undetected, component of the economic scene is the 'grey economy' which entails economic activities which are typically captured in the national income figures, but which are either illicit in a technical sense, or stand in a grey area on legal grounds. It is not clear, therefore, whether they should be regarded from an economics-and-law perspective as comprising part of the formal economy or the black economy. One pertinent example is that of the status of Sunday trading in non-exempt items in England and Wales in the years from the mid-to-late 1980s onwards, when it became increasingly unclear – until the ruling of the ECJ on the *Stoke-on-Trent* case in 1993 (as explained in Section II, above, p.22) – whether or not the prohibition against Sunday trading contained in the Shops Act 1950 was conformable or not with Article 30 of the Treaty of Rome.

The existence of the grey economy is almost entirely ignored in much economic analysis but it probably comprises surprisingly large volumes of economic activity.[81] New and

---

81 To give an example, in the court disputes in the late 1980s surrounding the question of the proportionality of the Shops Act 1950, I and other expert witnesses were led to construct estimates of the volume of EC trade caught by these regulations applying to England and Wales. On the most conservative assumptions (in retrospect) we came to the general conclusion that around ECU 1 billion (£750 million approximately) was involved.

complex regulations issuing from government (and supranational governments/agencies such as the EC) create wide scope for grey areas in legal and commercial interpretation. There is a more detailed discussion of the grey economy in Appendix 1 (below, pp.89-92).

The concept of the grey economy is relevant to the debate over the options for the reform of Sunday trading law in England and Wales because (as elaborated in Section IV) the KSSC model rests upon vague concepts of what a shop's 'principal activity' is/what its business is 'wholly or mainly', whereas the RSAR model now rests upon the even vaguer approach of allowing the courts to decide a shop's main activity. All of these formulations would be open to much legal disputation in the courts, with the consequence that both local authorities and retailers would be unclear about the content and applicability of the regulations in the case of particular shops. The courts in turn would have to struggle with complex matters of business policy – such as what array of functional strategies (ranging from store layout to stocking policy and 'design ambience') is consistent with the stipulated formulation. This would give endless employment to lawyers and to expert witnesses they hire from business schools. It is also, however, a classic recipe for turning Sunday trading into a major area for 'grey' economic activity, with considerable costs for retailers, local authorities and, ultimately, shoppers and taxpayers.

Other Costs of Regulation

In general, all regulation involves a cost to taxpayers via additions to the burden of the public sector. An equally, perhaps more, significant hidden cost is thrown upon households and the market sector of the formal economy because their opportunities for efficient collaboration (e.g., in the activity of shopping) are reduced. There is, moreover, an even more invisible cost involved – a diversion of entrepreneurial talent amongst producers into finding ways around the regulations via legal loopholes and other devices, and away from more productive pursuits.[82]

---

82 This – and other – social costs of a regulatory régime via the effects upon entrepreneurial endeavour are explored in detail by I.M. Kirzner, *op. cit.*, Ch.6: 'The Perils of Regulation: A Market-Process Analysis'.

Such costs could be avoided by deregulation. Indeed, as the foregoing discussion underlines, what really is involved is more aptly termed the *decriminalisation* of this type of trading between willing buyers and willing sellers. The 'regulation' of Sunday is in reality an attempt to criminalise a non-coercive exchange activity (which has none of the problems associated with, for example, trading in hard drugs). One fundamental aspect of the case for deregulation of Sunday trading is that it is not an area in which the criminal law should be made to apply in a free society.

4. Conclusion: Further Prospects of Retail Revolution?

This Section has elaborated the foundations of the arguments for deregulating Sunday trading on a number of grounds, emphasising particularly the long-run, evolutionary aspects. It cannot be emphasised enough that these evolutionary forces are unpredictable.

Some of the changes in progress in the retailing industry give some clue to the shape of things to come. In the USA, the number of 'warehouse club' operations (whereby consumers pay an annual membership fee to buy goods at wholesale prices) has doubled within about three years – and this new format has just arrived in the UK.[83] Earlier in this Section the ongoing fast development of corner-store 'deep discounter' retail formats in the UK was noted. Also, the ex-jewellery retailer Mr Gerald Ratner is simultaneously unveiling plans to open 'factory outlet shopping malls' in this country (another retail concept imported from the USA).[84] Furthermore, some new developments could revolutionise shopping:

'At home, a scanner passed over store cupboards could build up a shopping list to be sent, say each month, to a central store by phone. The store would deliver the shopping to the door, plus any extra items keyed in on a computer pad.'[85]

---

83 'American Food Retailers: No Picnic', *Economist*, 17 July 1993, p.66. A High Court ruling of 27 October 1993 struck down the attempted legal blockage (by some UK retailers) of the entry to the British market by Costco, a major US warehouse club. Costco's first UK facility opened in Thurrock, Essex, on 30 November 1993.

84 N. Fletcher, 'Ratner's Return', *Sunday Express*, 24 July 1993, p.49.

85 S. Poulter, 'Good Buy To All That', *Daily Mail*, 24 June 1993, p.23.

Such ideas are not in the realms of science fiction. In 1993 Andersen Consulting is opening a 'Smart Store Europe' in a £3 million complex near Windsor, to demonstrate new advances in shopping technology. One possible development is that 'shops' will emerge with no check-out staff whatsoever (and indeed a check-out free store is already being tested in Holland by the Albert Heign Company).[86] Inevitably, any new set of 'polished and updated' regulations, based upon business formats as they are *now*, will become outmoded over time – perhaps more rapidly than we perceive.

---

86 For a survey of present home-shopping/teleshopping business in the EC, see
    E. Ploch and P. Brook, 'Shopping Sans Frontieres? European Integration and
    Home Shopping', *European Business and Economic Development*, Vol.1, No.2.,
    September 1992, pp.7-12. This 'map' of present arrangements could be
    greatly transformed by the new technology.

VI. CONCERNS ABOUT DEREGULATION

Critics of the deregulation approach to Sunday trading commonly concede there may be a case on 'market' grounds for the removal of trading restrictions, but then go on to argue that other substantial considerations must be addressed. In economic terminology such objections are variants of a 'market failure' argument – the proposition that market forces fail to generate an 'ideal' outcome, and that government intervention (in this case, restrictions on Sunday trading) is necessary to correct the outcome of market forces.

This Section examines three central concerns about alleged market failure which have been raised by proponents of both the KSSC and RSAR models. They are, *first*, concerns about the survival of small shops and shopkeepers in the light of trends to concentration in certain sectors of UK retailing; *second*, concerns about spillovers (noise, congestion, and so on) generated by an extension of Sunday trading in England and Wales; and, *third*, concerns about shop employee income, employment and family welfare.

The Small Shop and Concentration in Retailing

The survival of the small shop is often argued to be an important goal of public policy on grounds such as: the importance of family businesses as sources of entrepreneurial talent and training; the convenience of small shops to customers (especially the young and the old); and the importance of small shops to village and rural life and also to the 'traditional' high street.

Simultaneously, there has been concern about the concentration of retailing into the 'big battalions' of the multiples. It is argued that deregulation of Sunday trading would tip the balance even further in this direction, allowing chains and big-store retailers to expand even more at the expense of small traders. Indeed, in the most pessimistic formulation, Sunday trading deregulation (full or partial) might substantially 'wipe out' the small shops sector.

An underlying goal of the RSAR proposals, in particular, is to preserve the structure of the retailing industry against the further unleashing of such market forces.

[72]

Long-term Decline of the Small Shop?

The small shop has certainly been in decline over the post-war period in the UK. In 1950, when the Shops Act was passed, most retail goods were bought in small shops, typically located near customers' homes from behind-counter staff. Self-service was untypical, and indeed large stores were not prominent. Even by 1961 the multiples accounted for only 28·2 per cent of total retail turnover in the UK. By 1984, however, the market share of the multiples had risen to over half of total retail trade.

The continuation of such pressures in the 1980s is illustrated in Table 2, which shows that the market share of single-outlet food shops fell over this period (though that of single-outlet non-food shops *rose*). The share of large multiples increased considerably in both sectors.

Decline was most marked in the case of the small owner-managed *village* shop, rather than the urban corner shop where there was a steady injection over the post-war period of new entrepreneurial talent from the ethnic minorities, and particularly the Asian community. In England in 1970, there were around 40,000 village shops; it is estimated that by 1990 there were only some 8,000 remaining.[87] The *general* decline of the small shop has been less marked: the number of non-food single outlets actually *rose* by 7 per cent over the 1980s, even though there was a fall

TABLE 2

CHANGING MARKET SHARES IN UK RETAILING, 1980-89
Changes in retail turnover, at constant prices.

(*per cent*)

Type of Shop	Food	Non-Food	Total
Single Outlets	-20	+19	+7
Large Multiples	+35	+47	+42
Total	+16	+31	+25

Source: London Economics, 1993

---

87 'Not all Roses', *Economist*, 24 February 1990, p.34.

TABLE 3
STRUCTURAL CHANGE IN UK RETAILING, 1980-89
(*per cent*)

Type of Shop	Food	Non-Food	Total
Single Outlets	-25	+7	-5
Large Multiples	-32	+13	+1
Total	-26	+5	-5

Source: London Economics, 1993

in the number of all single outlets in UK retailing of some 5 per cent over that decade (Table 3).

It is to be noted, however, that restrictions on Sunday trading were in effect in England and Wales throughout the period in which the small shop declined. The Shops Act 1950 did not stem that downward curve.

Nor would adoption of the KSSC or RSAR models be likely to reverse the trend since the growth of the multiples has been but one cause in a more general set of forces leading to a thinning of the ranks of small shops. Undoubtedly the upgrading of store facilities in multiple outlets (compared with small shops) over the past 40 years has been a factor changing market shares of single outlets and the multiples, as has been the attraction of 'one-stop' shopping in an environment in which the opportunity cost of time was increasing. There have, however, been other forces at work such as changes in consumer preferences, the emergence of shopping as a leisure activity and, in particular, the massive post-war rise in car ownership – greatly enhancing the ability of consumers to do bulk shopping on a one-stop basis at a multiple outlet.

It is not at all clear how the retention or intensification of Sunday trading restrictions along the lines of the KSSC/RSAR models would combat these other forces. Indeed, the strict enforcement of either model would most likely reduce the prospects of those small shops which would be forced to close on Sundays (see boxes E and F, above, pp.43 and 46).

It is, in any case, extremely unlikely that the small shop is on the way to complete extinction. There will always be a demand for local convenience shopping of 'forgotten and 'top-up' items missed out from the supermarket trolley. If anything, the demand for such local shops is likely to *grow* with the 'greying' of the age-structure of the population towards more retired people (who are less likely or able to drive than pre-retirement consumers). As noted earlier (see Section V, sub-section (iii)), the European evidence would indicate that this is indeed occurring. It would appear that in the EC as a whole the supermarket and superstore formats have reached a mature (or perhaps declining) stage, whilst small convenience stores in inner cities are in a growth phase.

Concentration and Competition in Retailing

There remains the question of concentration in retailing, which has been particularly marked in food retailing. By March 1992 the four biggest chains in this area of retailing – Tesco, Sainsbury, Asda and Safeway – accounted for some 32.4 per cent of the UK food retail market.[88]

It is likely that (other things equal) deregulation of Sunday trading could increase the market concentration ratio in at least certain sectors of UK retailing where there are as yet unexploited economies of scale and scope. It is, indeed, a central assumption of the (closely conceptually allied) econometric retailing models developed by the IFS in 1984 and London Economics in 1993 that deregulation would lead to some expansion of larger stores in the long run.[89] In their models, Sunday trading deregulation acts to increase the capacity of the retailing industry. This (it is assumed) is not matched by a like increase in the short run in overall consumer retail expenditure, leading to a short-run downward pressure on retail profit margins. This in turn leads to structural change in the industry, until the excess capacity is reduced:

> '...by means of a more rapid closure of secondary units and reduced investment in new stores by the stronger traders, and by exit from the industry by weaker ones. For these reasons, longer opening hours [and Sunday trading deregulation] probably accelerate the

---

88 S. Fairbairn, 'Times are Tough at the Tills of Tesco', *Financial Times*, 22 September 1992, p.31.

89 See earlier citations.

[75]

trend towards the disappearance from the marketplace of independent traders and towards increasing concentration amongst multiple retailers.'[90]

Equilibrium is restored in this model once unit costs have been sufficiently lowered that profit margins return to 'normal'. The process is, however, not without benefit to consumers in terms of lower prices (as efficiency gains are passed on).

Assuming this model to be correct (for the sake of argument), is there legitimate ground for worry about the presumed concentration-enforcing character of Sunday trading deregulation?

In answering that question, the following points are relevant. *First*, Sunday trading deregulation would add only a relatively small once-over impetus to trends that prevail for other reasons. *Second*, the retailing industry will remain vigorously competitive, not least because of the existence of low barriers to entry. Indeed, as recorded in Section V, we are currently witnessing a major new form of entry in UK food retailing: 'traditional' British food retailing chains are under competitive attack by Continental invaders deploying a 'deep-discounting' strategy, and US-style warehouse clubs are also on their way. *Third*, the car-based mobility of consumers noted earlier in this Section also disciplines large retailers in local markets in a way that was not true (say) 40 years ago. Consequently, there is good reason to believe that the strength of the competitive process in UK retailing means there need be no serious concern about the minor additional impulses to concentration in some sections of the retailing industry that might result from Sunday trading deregulation.

Moreover, as argued in the London Economics 1993 study, *if* there is concern about any alleged lack of competition in the retailing industry, then the appropriate policy avenue is for these matters to be referred to the Monopolies and Mergers Commission for investigation. Seeking to argue for the retention or reinforcement of Sunday trading laws so as to 'increase competition' would be a roundabout way of going about such matters! On the contrary (and as suggested in Section II), historically Sunday trading laws have been lobbied

---

90   London Economics Study, 1993, *op. cit.*, p.3.

for by retail groups with a direct interest in *inhibiting* competition.

Sunday 'Spillovers'

It has been argued that deregulation of Sunday trading would create serious negative external effects – in the form of extra noise and congestion – for the residents of shopping areas affected by new Sunday shop opening. Additionally, council taxpayers could be faced with additional costs in the form of extra policing, street cleaning and refuse collection, and (subsidies to) public transport as a result of an 'open Sunday' in England and Wales.

The Auld Committee admitted in its 1984 report that this complex of spillover factors could be 'a matter for real concern'[91] (though it went on to advocate full deregulation). It is a concern that will doubtless resurface in the contemporary debate over the reform of Sunday trading law in England and Wales.

What Net Effect?

Any increased cost of the sort described above will depend on the overall volume of new trade generated by full deregulation. Economists disagree about this matter. Some assume that total deregulation of Sunday trading on the lines of the Scottish model would add to overall retail activity in a small but positive fashion.[92] Others assume, as in the base or central assumption of the 1984 IFS study and the 1993 London Economics retail models, that such deregulation would not add significantly to overall retail activity; it would simply redistribute the trade over the week.

Whichever is the case, no doubt a considerable volume of Sunday trading would result from consumers redistributing their purchases over time to avail themselves of new Sunday shopping opportunities. Thus, to a considerable degree, whilst congestion and other costs might rise on Sundays, there would be an offsetting *reduction* in such costs on weekdays. Whilst weekend working in the public services (as elsewhere) tends to be at premium rates, there is thus a large element of 'swings and roundabouts' in this matter.

---

91 Auld Report, *op. cit.*, para.170.
92 T. Burke and J.R. Shackleton, *op. cit.*

Moreover, as argued in Section II, a considerable amount of adjustment to Sunday trading has already taken place in England and Wales, as the Shops Act has fallen into abeyance in many local authority areas.

It also has to be remembered that 'shopping trips are only a small proportion of all journeys, and many offices and service outlets are likely to remain closed on Sunday even if a large proportion of retail outlets do open'.[93] Moreover, as the opportunity cost of Sunday time lost because of congestion is likely to be less to the average traveller than during a weekday, there is an offsetting cost reduction factor. Finally, since there is already a degree of *de facto* deregulation of Sunday trading, the likelihood is that *re*-regulation under the KSSC or RSAR models would have contrary redistributive effects which would entail extra costs, by increasing the volume of weekday and Saturday trading and shopping trips.

On balance it seems likely that the net impact of Sunday trading deregulation (both the external and fiscal costs, compared with those resulting from alternative regulatory régimes) would be minimal.

Some Evidence

Evidence collected by the Auld Committee in 1984 is relevant. They examined the effects of total deregulation, and took evidence on these points from the Association of District Councils, the Association of Metropolitan Councils, the Association of County Councils, and a number of major individual local authorities. Their conclusion was that, in respect of local taxpayer costs arising from full deregulation of Sunday trading:

> 'The balance of informed evidence suggests that there would be no significant increase in the burden of expenditure on [local] public services.'[94]

The Committee concluded that 'any increase in the costs of public services would be likely to be trivial, and certainly not such as to justify the retention of the restriction on trading hours'.[95]

---

93 London Economics Study, 1993, *op. cit.*, p.48.

94 Auld Report, para.173.

95 Auld Report, para.179.

This conclusion is not altered by more recent evidence collected by London Economics in 1993, which involved information from four local authorities (Lincoln, Sutton, Kirklees and Blackpool) chosen with a view to providing a balanced sample of authorities which adopt a 'permissive' and a 'strict' line on the enforcement of the existing régime of Sunday trading law.

The case against deregulation on grounds of the allegedly substantial spillover and public costs entailed is therefore, on the evidence to hand, at least not proven. Moreover, as argued in Section V, the regulatory approaches of the KSSC and RSAR models would undoubtedly add in some degree to the enforcement costs burdening local authorities on this account, not least because of the nebulous nature of the definition of a shop's business that is central to these schemes (see Section III and Section V, sub-section (v)). Indeed, it has to be remembered that – as the London Economics evidence reveals – 'attempts to enforce the Shops Act have been costly' to many councils.[96]

The foregoing matters are underscored by the results of a recent survey of the attitudes of over 200 councils to the four options for the reform of Sunday trading conducted by the Institute of Public Finance (IPF).[97] This study found that as regards the costs of enforcing the four alternatives, full deregulation was the first or second choice of 92.6 per cent of those surveyed, whilst the SHRC model attracted 59.4 per cent of these first or second preferences. By contrast, the KSSC and RSAR models obtained only 11.4 per cent and 8.8 per cent (of first or second preferences) respectively.

The more surprising element of the IPF study is the revealed attitude of councillors to the cost of other services (such as traffic control and litter collection) likely to be involved in the implementation of the four models. The charge against the deregulatory models by their critics is that their adoption would significantly add to such costs. Yet the IPF study found that, even on these grounds, the deregulation option was the first or second preference of 79.4 per cent, whilst the SHRC model achieved 54.8 per cent of these preferences. Again in contrast, the KSSC model was favoured

96 London Economics Study, 1993, *op. cit.*, p.41.

97 P. Ramsdale and A. Kapaldi, *Sunday Trading: A Study of the Impact on Local Authorities*, London: IPF, October 1993.

on grounds of these public costs by only 23.9 per cent, and the RSAR by only 18.7 per cent, in terms of the cumulative rankings (that is, either first or second) of those surveyed.

In the light of these findings, it is – to say the least – difficult to sustain the case against the deregulation of Sunday trading in terms of the alleged cost burden that it would pose for local authorities.

Concerns About Shopworkers

One element in the KSSC case for the retention and updating/intensification of Sunday trading regulations in England and Wales is concern for the conditions of shop employees. The contention is that Sunday trading deregulation would in a number of ways harm the interests of such workers. Their employment prospects and remuneration would suffer; full-time shop employees would be replaced by part-time 'Sundays-only' workers; and employees would be coerced into working on Sundays in order to retain their jobs.

Compulsion to Work on Sunday?

The Government's draft legislation contains clauses specially protecting those already in retail employment against being compelled to work on Sundays if this is against their wishes.[98] Moreover, a study of Sunday workers in 452 superstores (drawn from the DIY and grocery sectors) conducted in 1992 by members of the Institute of Retail Studies at Stirling University, pointed to a 'high level of acceptance of and willingness to work on Sundays, based mainly on financial reasons'.[99]

There might, even accepting this evidence of the generally voluntary nature of Sunday working in the retail trade, be concerns about the effects of such work on the family life of shop employees. The Stirling survey of Sunday Retail Employees, however, found that:

> 'Most respondents also had no children (54 per cent). The survey points to the Sunday workforce being predominantly female and young but with a high percentage [also] of young, male shopfloor workers'.[100]

---

98 See above, Section III, p.33.

99 P. Freathy and L. Sparks, 'Sunday Working in the Retail Trade', University of Stirling: Institute of Retail Studies, 1992 (mimeo), p.7.

100 *Ibid.*, p.5.

Moreover, the Spring 1992 Labour Force Survey indicated that some '40 per cent of the British working population either sometimes or usually works on a Sunday'.[101] Concern about the family life of Sunday workers cannot, therefore, be addressed by any measure such as Sunday trading legislation that concentrates upon the retail trade alone.

Thus the balance of evidence, coupled with the government guarantee in respect of Sunday rights for current retail workers, suggests that there is a much weaker basis for concern about these aspects of Sunday trading deregulation than its opponents imply.

Effects of Deregulation on
Retail Employment and Wage Prospects

Perhaps the nub of the concerns – at least as viewed from a trade union perspective – relates more to the impact of Sunday trading deregulation on the job and wage prospects of shop employees.

The simulation results using the retailing model (described above) of London Economics led to the conclusion that implementation of the full deregulation model would result in a (long-run) job loss of (almost) 20,000 (other things equal), combined with a marginal increase in average retail wages of around 1·2 per cent (the largest overall wage increase to shop employees generated by any of the options, in their evaluation).[102]

Such estimated job losses are small compared with the sheer scale of the retail sector; they would account for about 1·5 per cent of the present retail workforce. Moreover, they would be spread over many years, during which time many other developments are likely to take place. Thus, the deregulation of Sunday trading would be likely to alter the structure of the retail workforce only marginally. As one of the members of the Auld Committee recently noted: '...there would be an acceleration of the long-term trend towards the employment of more women and more part-timers in the industry'.[103] But, as she also emphasises: '...what would

---

101 Cm. 2300, para.6.

102 London Economics Study, 1993, *op. cit.*, p.37.

103 F. Cairncross, 'Shopping Hours: The Options for Reform', London: Special Lecture at Royal Institute of Chartered Surveyors, 18 June 1992 (mimeo), p.9.

happen is the acceleration of an existing trend rather than a new one'.[104]

Given the relatively small – not to say minuscule – size of the anticipated effects (both on employment and wages), this concern about deregulation also seems exaggerated. Indeed, with a considerable number of retail employees already working on Sundays, an intensification of Sunday trading restrictions under the KSSC or RSAR models would have the immediate effect of reducing employment in retailing.

These contrary concerns – fears about job losses resulting from the re-regulation of Sunday trading in England and Wales via implementation of the KSSC or RSAR models – may have considerably undermined 'traditional' union opposition to deregulation. It is reported, for example, that there has been disagreement in USDAW's ranks about the union's long and staunch opposition to deregulatory models, which '...follows meetings with Tesco staff – a quarter of the membership – who have demanded the right to work on Sundays'.[105] This may explain the dramatic shift in USDAW's position as regards Sunday trading matters announced on 1 November 1993. Historically (as discussed in Section II), USDAW has been a bastion of support for the KSSC, and a major lobby against all parliamentary attempts to reform the Shops Act 1950 in a deregulatory direction, over the intervening decades. The union's newly announced position is that, 'given the changing views of its members', it no longer supports the KSSC model. Moreover, although it remains opposed to full deregulation, it would be prepared to throw its weight behind the SHRC model (if accompanied by certain other conditions).[106]

---

104 *Ibid.*, p.9. The long-term trend to the greater utilisation of part-time employees, prominent not only in retailing but throughout industry and commerce generally, is examined in T. Walsh, 'Part-time Employment and Labour Market Policies', *National Westminster Bank Quarterly Review*, May 1989, pp.43-55.

105 A. Law, 'Biggest Shop Union Makes a U-Turn Over Sunday Trading', *Sunday Express*, 11 July 1993, p.15. It has also been reported that the GMB (one of the UK's largest unions) has recently written to its 31 sponsored Labour MPs asking them to support Sunday shopping deregulation: see *Sunday Shopper*, January 1993, p.2.

106 These conditions are that all shopworkers (both current and future) would have the right to opt out of Sunday working, and that the (statutory) premium for Sunday retail work is double the standard (weekday) rate. (*Source:* USDAW press release, 1 November 1993.)

It remains the case, however, that retailing is a relatively low-paid area of the economy and so there may be legitimate grounds for general concern about low pay in this industry. Opposition to Sunday trading deregulation on such grounds is, however, wrong-headed. *First*, the econometric evidence noted above – though it should be treated with caution – indicates that deregulation offers most potential of all of the reform options for boosting average retail wages (albeit only very marginally). *Second*, the appropriate response to low-pay problems is not trading restrictions inflicted on one specific industry, but rather general policies to improve the supply-side of the economy and to enhance the prospects of low-paid workers generally.

Conclusion

In a mature and tolerant free society, government should not come between the voluntary arrangements and exchanges desired by its citizens, unless some clear and substantive public harm can be demonstrated. This Section has examined three concerns that have been voiced about allowing full freedom for retailers and shoppers to trade on Sundays in England and Wales, as in Scotland.

The arguments supporting such concerns have been shown to be, at the least, weak. On such grounds there is no substantial case for the continued regulation of Sunday trading.

If this conclusion is, however, rejected it follows that it should be rejected also north of the Border. What is good for the English goose cannot *simultaneously* be deemed wrong for the Scottish gander.

VII. THE POLITICAL ECONOMY
OF SUNDAY TRADING REFORM

This *Hobart Paper* has examined the options for reform of Sunday trading law in England and Wales and the historical and legal background to this longstanding and vexed matter. It argues on various economic grounds that one particular option – full deregulation of Sunday trading in England and Wales in line with the long-established situation in Scotland – is the correct policy choice.

The Auld Committee received a huge volume of evidence – over 7,300 submissions – from business organisations, trade unions, local authorities, churches and trade associations. Despite the conflicting views expressed, the Committee came to the same clear conclusion at the end of their lengthy investigations and exhaustive report as that earlier argued by Ralph Harris and Arthur Seldon:[107]

> '...we recommend the abolition in England, Wales and Scotland of all legal restrictions on the hours for which shops may be open to serve customers.'[108]

As outlined in Section II, when the Auld Report was initially debated in the House of Commons, there was a majority of 120 in favour of its recommendations. Subsequently, however, the Bill based upon that report was rejected by a small majority of the House. A 'temporary' Act of Parliament – the Shops Act, 1950, widely acknowledged as anachronistic, riddled with anomalies and ripe for reform – had survived another attempt to repeal it, despite the clear arguments against the Act and its public unpopularity.

Public opinion polls in England and Wales continue to testify to the dominant majority in favour of Sunday trading deregulation. The fabric of Part IV of the Shops Act 1950 is even more tattered than it was in 1983, with quite widespread disregard (said to include even Buckingham Palace)[109] for

---

107 R. Harris and A. Seldon, *Shoppers' Choice: An Essay in the Political Economy of Obstruction by Sectional Interests to the Repeal of the Shops Acts*, Occasional Paper 68, London: Institute of Economic Affairs, 1984.

108 Auld Report, 1984, para.291.

109 R. Wilsher, 'Palace Breaks Sunday Laws: Royal Gift Shop Sells Goods on Banned List', *Sunday Express*, 8 August 1993, p.1.

this antiquated law. And yet, in January 1993, 214 MPs (nearly one-third of the House) voted for the Powell Bill, which was the predecessor of the present KSSC/RSAR regulatory options. (Thus one has the feeling of a sense of *déja vu*, as so often on this subject!) An amalgam of special interests may again obstruct a popular reform.

What explains this continuing gulf between popular aspiration on the one hand, and the government's slowness to act on the other? Why may the deregulation of Sunday trading continue to face (perhaps predominant) political opposition? Some answers may be found in the economic analysis of regulation.

The Transitional Gains Trap

Section II explained that the original impetus towards Sunday trading regulation in the 1930s was closely associated with concentrations of trade association and trade union interests that lobbied for these restrictions.

Once passed into law, the restrictions generate supra-normal returns for those interests which promoted them.[110] However, these high returns are likely to prove temporary for the interests involved. Moreover, any attempt to repeal the restriction will generate short-run losses for the beneficiaries; they have a vested interest in opposing reform. Consequently, the political system, once induced to grant groups special privileges (for example, against competition or by subsidy), faces vociferous opposition to their removal at a later date. A ratchet effect occurs.

Professor Gordon Tullock, who first diagnosed the problem, called it the 'transitional gains trap'.[111] There are many examples ranging from the Common Agricultural Policy of the EC to the taxi 'medallion' system of cab licensing in New York City.

A particular example used by Professor Tullock in his original exposition was the case of the so-called 'Blue Laws' in the USA – the equivalent of the Sunday trading laws in

---

110 Technically, to the economist, this supra-normal return is known as a 'rent', and the activity of searching for such gains via the manipulation of (primarily) the political market is termed 'rent-seeking' in economic analysis.

111 G. Tullock, 'The Transitional Gains Trap', *Bell Journal of Economics*, Vol.6, Autumn 1975, pp.671-78; reprinted in J.M. Buchanan and R.D. Tollison (eds.), *Towards a Theory of the Rent Seeking Society*, College Station: Texas A & M University Press, 1980, pp.211-21.

England and Wales. Tullock's underlying economic model is exactly the same as that utilised by the IFS in 1984 and London Economics in 1993 to model prospective changes in retail opening hours in the UK. The imposition of new Sunday trading laws is equivalent to a reduction in industry capacity (just as subsequent deregulation would represent an increase in capacity, other things being equal). The capacity reduction causes a temporary increase in profits and wages, although at the cost of short-run store closure and unemployment of retail workers who might otherwise have remained employed).[112]

The government-induced reduction in retail industry capacity consequent upon the introduction (or intensification) of Sunday trading laws leads to a temporary rise in profits, and then to new capacity construction over the medium to longer run. The outcome is that

> 'we … have the situation in which there are more stores than there were before and the return on all the stores is, once again, normal. The customers are not being served quite so well, so we have a social cost. … On the other hand, although the store owners are now making normal profits, the repeal of the Blue Laws [i.e. Sunday trading restrictions] would be quite inconvenient for them … they would suffer a considerable transitional loss.'[113]

The existence of a transitional gains trap may explain part of the political effort devoted to the retention and indeed intensification of Sunday trading regulations in England and Wales. But it is, perhaps, not the entire story. Two other elements seem particularly relevant: attempts to overcome the process of 'intervention entropy', and the problem of 'intertwined interests'.

Battling Against Intervention Entropy

'Intervention entropy' arises because government regulations become less effective over time as evasion and avoidance build up, new loopholes emerge, and new 'grey areas' for regulation come into being because economic evolution throws up 'problems', products and contracts not conceived

---

112 The scenario that would be involved in England and Wales upon implementation of either the KSSC or RSAR models.

113 Tullock, *op. cit.*, pp.215-16.

of when the original regulatory measure was formulated. In short, 'anomalies' and grey/black economy substitution are bound to build up over time.

One response to such intervention entropy[114] is a rejigging of regulation to try to take account of the new problems faced by the old regulatory measures. In other words, political pressure will emerge for a 'polishing and updating' of the regulatory framework in order to battle against intervention entropy.

The Problem of Intertwined Interests

Much modern public choice analysis presumes that regulation is promulgated by narrow sectional economic interests and benefits those interests. It is indeed difficult to think of regulations which have endured over time which have *not* had the support of powerful organised interests. An interesting hypothesis is that the coalition of apparently different interest groups – supporting a regulation on diverse grounds ranging from the ostensibly moral to the basest consideration of competitive strategy – may make for the most entrenched restrictions/regulations of all (at whatever injury to wider economic interests).[115] Two or more disparate lobbies have a political synergy that would be absent if they were not so combined. Political and economic history suggests that most attempts at restricting competition have depended for their long-run survival upon the tandem of continued governmental support and a 'reasonable' cover in terms of their supposed social justification based on quasi-moralistic grounds.

Conclusions

The survival of Sunday trading restrictions in England and Wales constitutes a major political paradox. These restrictions are generally regarded as anachronistic. They are also widely flouted. Public opinion polls show a big majority in favour of

---

114 An analysis of the process of intervention entropy and its sources is in J. Burton, 'The Instability of the Middle Way', in N. Barry *et al.*, *Hayek's 'Serfdom' Revisited*, Hobart Paperback No.18, London: Institute of Economic Affairs, 1984.

115 Discussed in B. Yandle, 'Intertwined Interests, Rent Seeking and Regulation', *Social Science Quarterly*, Vol.65, December 1984, pp.1,004-12, and J. Price and B. Yandle, 'Labor Markets and Sunday Closing Laws', *Journal of Labor Research*, Vol.8, No.4, Fall 1987, pp.407-14.

their abandonment. Nevertheless, it has proved 'politically impossible', so far, to remove this arcane and much derided set of regulations which is sustained by the political and regulatory process.

Attempts to refresh and intensify these regulatory measures are now on the agenda – and could well become the law of the land. The implementation of either the KSSC or RSAR models would, however, create many other new paradoxes. To misquote Ralph Waldo Emerson, if a shop of 270 square metres is selling a mousetrap on a Sunday morning then the world will be allowed to beat a path to its door. But if a shop of 290 square metres is to do the same thing – or even to sell a better mousetrap – then its doors might be closed by court injunction, whether or not shoppers want to beat a path there.

The case made by this *Hobart Paper* is that the criminal law should be applied in matters where serious and indisputable public evil is involved. Conversely, criminal law should *not* be applied to mundane transactions between willing participants in which no public harm is involved. The argument for deregulating Sunday trading in England and Wales is that such ordinary – and currently extensive – shopping transactions *should be decriminalised*. It is no part of the state's job in a free society to interfere with these transactions – let alone apply to them the full weight of the criminal law.

APPENDIX 1

The Grey Economy

The double-headed arrowlines *A*, *B* and *C* in Figure 1 represent avenues or pathways of interchange and substitution between the three economies in the traditional triad. The grey economy stands 'somewhere' between the formal economy and the black economy in this particular avenue of substitution (labelled as *B*); it is a borderland arena of economic activity which is being continuously redefined by the emergence of new economic regulations and thus new legal uncertainties regarding commercial activity.

The confident assumption of much economic analysis, until relatively recently, was that the main avenue of substitution and interchange between the three economies is that labelled *A*; and that it was primarily in a one-way direction. The 'process of industrialisation' was supposed to lead undirectionally to the increasing replacement of the self-service economy by the formal economy. Since the work of Gershuny economists have realised that the substitutions along this avenue are far more complex – and that, in particular, the self-service economy (since the 1950s) in many instances has been displacing the formal economy (as with the massive growth of self-service shopping over this period).[1] More generally, all of the depicted avenues of substitution and interchange between the three economies are operative, ongoing, and occur in a two-way direction.

The Effects of Regulation

In terms of the schema developed in Section IV, imposition of a Sunday trading regulatory régime upon a previously-unregulated situation would have four general effects:

(i) New impediments are created to the two-way interchange along avenue *A* between the household economy and the formal economy ('shopping'), and the future possibilities of evolution in this regard.

---

[1]   J.I. Gershuny, *Social Innovation and the Division of Labour*, Oxford: Oxford University Press, 1983.

Figure 1: Relations between Economies

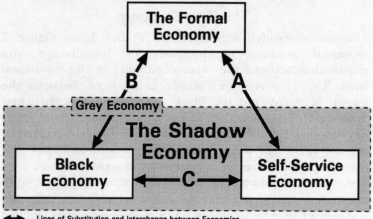

Lines of Substitution and Interchange between Economies
Adapted from: S. Smith and S. Weid-Nebbeling, *The Shadow Economy in Britain and Germany*, London: A

(ii) An incentive is created to develop two-way interchanges along avenue *C* (for retailers to serve shoppers illicitly on a Sunday).

(iii) There is also likely to be some diversion of activity from the formal economy into the 'grey' economy along avenue *B* (this effect depending upon the complexity and lack of clarity of the regulatory schema).

(iv) There will also be some alteration in the composition of the formal economy. Whilst (other things equal) the size of the market sector of the formal economy is reduced, due to effects noted under headings (i), (ii) and (iii), there will be some increase in the public sector component of the formal economy resulting from the necessity to monitor, staff and enforce the new regulations. The extent of this increase in the public sector will depend on such factors as the degree of popular acceptance of (and thus compliance with) the new regulations, the severity of penalties for transgression, and the willingness of political authorities to

[90]

utilise taxpayer funds to enforce these regulations given other, perhaps more pressing, calls upon the public purse.[2]

Two Regulatory Scenarios

The precise impact of any particular regulatory régime will depend upon its nature and content. To examine these matters we explore two stylised regulatory régimes and their impacts, which may be called Scenarios I and II.

In Scenario I we assume a Sunday trading regulatory régime of a complex nature with positive levels of penalty for transgression but which are relatively low compared to those of Scenario II. Assume also that there is haphazard enforcement activity ranging from the strict to the relaxed, depending upon local authority policy priorities. Assume also a degree of popular confusion about, and disregard for, the content of the regulations on the part of both many shoppers and retailers.

In terms of the framework developed above we would expect this scenario to involve an outcome with extensive diversion of Sunday trading activity along avenues B and C into the black (and also possibly the grey) economy, and with some expansion of the public sector in comparison with a fully deregulated situation.

In Scenario II let us assume another regulatory régime of a complex nature combined with very much tougher penalties and a higher level of enforcement activity, but with some variation of this effort across local authorities. Assume also that the legal content of the regulations is open to interpretation and dispute in the courts.

In the latter scenario, the same general effects occur as in case I, but we would expect some elements of the outcome to

---

[2] The officials charged with enforcing the Shops Act 1950 in England and Wales are Trading Standards Officers; this duty would remain theirs under any new regulatory scheme for Sunday trading. These local authority officers also have quasi-police duties for (what many would regard as) more serious matters such as the detection and prevention of consumer fraud by retailers/self-employed professionals, and matters of food hygiene in shops and restaurants. The effort allocated by them currently under the Shops Act 1950 to Sunday trading regulation is determined by local authority policy. This would continue to be the case under the implementation of either the KSSC, RSAR or SHRC models; it is not necessarily the case that local authorities would regard these matters as of high priority (unless central government funded any additional expenditures involved).

differ quantitatively. Due to the deterrent effect of high penalty and enforcement levels, the impediments to interchange along avenue *A* would be significant, but the diversion of Sunday trading into the black economy along path *C* might well be less than in Scenario I (although it is unlikely to be zero due to the spotty nature of the enforcement levels – and indeed significant in those areas where local authorities are prepared to 'turn a blind eye' to illicit Sunday trading). The diversion of Sunday trading into the grey economy could, however, be *even more extensive* than in case I – the extent of this depending on the degree of 'greyness' and lack of clarity in the content of the regulatory régime.

TOPICS/QUESTIONS FOR DISCUSSION

1. 'There is no overwhelming purely economic argument in favour of or against regulation [of Sunday trading].' (Ben Laurance, 'Sunday Laws Still a Load of Tripe', *The Guardian*, 6 November 1993.) Discuss.

2. Evaluate the relevance of the concept of rent-seeking to the history and development of Sunday trading laws in England and Wales from the 1930s to the present.

3. Would it be possible to devise a régime for regulating Sunday trading that resulted in no distortions of competition? Discuss with relevance to both:

   (a) A short-run context in which the retail capital stock and the array of retail goods available may be assumed approximately constant; and

   (b) A long-run scenario in which it may be assumed that the retail capital stock is both variable and malleable, and that innovation is continuous.

4. Critically evaluate the validity of the simulation models of the retail industry that have been used by the IFS and London Economics to examine the effects of alternative Sunday trading regulatory régimes.

5. Examine the likely effects upon the prospects for small shops of the four options for the reform of Sunday trading law set out in Cm. 2300.

6. 'The dictum that competition is the optimum discovery procedure applies as much to the changing forms of retailing in the coming decades as to the hours for which existing shops open.' (R. Harris and A. Seldon, *Shoppers' Choice*, 1984). Discuss.

7. Sir James Blyth (chief executive of The Boots Company) wrote to all MPs on 9 November 1993 (in support of the

partial deregulation of Sunday trading in England and Wales), as follows:

> 'From a commercial point of view the arguments for and against Sunday trading are finely balanced. However, from the point of view of consumers and shopworkers we believe that there is an overwhelming case for Sunday opening to be deregulated, provided that certain safeguards apply.'

Evaluate the effects upon both consumers and shopworkers of the four models for reform in Cm. 2300, drawing upon Becker's theory of the allocation of time, and other relevant items of economic analysis and evidence. Do you reach the same conclusions (as regards consumer and shopworker welfare) as Sir James or not?

8. Explain the concept of 'the grey economy' and examine its relevance to the general debate about regulation *vs.* deregulation.

FURTHER READING

Official documents are often rather forbidding reading material. Students are advised that this is not true of the two crucial UK government publications on Sunday trading over the last decade:

Cmnd.9876, *The Shops Act: Late Night and Sunday Opening*, London: HMSO, November 1984 (commonly referred to as the Auld Report, after its chairman).

Cm.2300, *Reforming the Law on Sunday Trading: A Guide to the Options for Reform*, London: HMSO, July 1993.

o The case for the deregulation of Sunday trading has also been trenchantly put in:

Harris, R., and A. Seldon, *Shoppers' Choice*, London: Institute of Economic Affairs, Occasional Paper 68, 1984.

Burke, T., and J. R. Shackleton, *Sunday, Sunday: The Issues in Sunday Trading*, London: Adam Smith Institute, 1989. (This is especially valuable in drawing upon the American, Swedish and Scottish contexts.)

Hogbin, G., *Free to Shop*, St. Leonards, New South Wales: Centre for Independent Studies, 1983. (This paper provides an antipodean perspective on Sunday trading/shop hours.)

o Proponents of the KSSC model have also argued their case extensively in books and monographs, as in:

Townsend, C., and M. Schluter, *Why Keep Sunday Special?*, Cambridge: Jubilee Centre Publications, 1985.

Burton-Jones, S., *New Facts for Auld*, Cambridge: Jubilee Centre Publications, 1989.

o The law-and-economics aspects of the EC dimensions of Sunday trading are analysed in:

Askham, A.J., T. Burke, and D. Ramsden, *EC Sunday Trading*, London: Butterworths, 1990.

o Some of the same European legal ground (from a KSSC perspective) is covered in:

Jones, S., *Evidence on the European Sunday*, Cambridge: Jubilee Centre Publications, 1988.

o As regards the fundamental economic analysis on which this *Hobart Paper* has particularly drawn, students are especially recommended to read:

Becker, G.S., 'A Theory of the Allocation of Time', *Economic Journal*, Vol.75, No.3, September 1965, p.493.

Tullock, G., 'The Transitional Gains Trap', *Bell Journal of Economics*, Vol.6, Autumn 1975, pp.671-78.

Stigler, G.J., 'The Theory of Economic Regulation', *Bell Journal of Economics*, Vol.2, No.1, 1971.

Kirzner, I.M., *Discovery and the Capitalist Process*, Chicago: University of Chicago Press, 1985 (see especially Chapter 6: 'The Perils of Regulation: A Market-Process Analysis').